A MAP OF SIGNS AND SCENTS

AMJAD NASSER

A MAP OF SIGNS AND SCENTS

NEW AND SELECTED POEMS, 1979–2014

Translated from the Arabic by

Fady Joudah *and* Khaled Mattawa

CURBSTONE BOOKS

NORTHWESTERN UNIVERSITY PRESS

EVANSTON, ILLINOIS

Curbstone Books
Northwestern University Press
www.nupress.northwestern.edu

The poems "Exile," "Bent Branches," "Loneliness," "Fever," and "Shepherds of Solitude" were first published in *Shepherd of Solitude: Selected Poems 1979–2004*, by Banipal Books, an imprint of Banipal Publishing, London, in 2009. Original works in Arabic copyright © Amjad Nasser; English translation copyright © Khaled Mattawa. Reprinted by permission.

English translation for all other poems copyright © 2016 by Curbstone Books/Northwestern University Press. Published 2016. All rights reserved.

Printed in the United States of America

10 9 8 7 6 5 4 3 2 1

Library of Congress Cataloging-in-Publication Data

Names: Nāsir, Amjad, author. | Joudah, Fady, 1971– translator. | Mattawa, Khaled, translator.
Title: A map of signs and scents : new and selected poems, 1979–2014 / Amjad Nasser ;
    translated from the Arabic by Fady Joudah and Khaled Mattawa.
Description: Evanston, Illinois : Curbstone Books/Northwestern University Press, 2016.
Identifiers: LCCN 2016017484| ISBN 9780810133655 (pbk. : alk. paper) | ISBN
    9780810133662 (e-book)
Classification: LCC PJ7852.A677 A2 2016 | DDC 892.716—dc23
LC record available at https://lccn.loc.gov/2016017484

CONTENTS

ACKNOWLEDGMENTS

Special thanks to print and online journals in which some of these poems first appeared: *At Length*, *Banipal*, *PEN America*, *PN Review*, *POEM*, *World Literature Today*.

"Petra: The Concealed Rose" was originally commissioned by Riwaq Gallery in Amman, Jordan, and was first published as a chapbook with Tavern Books, 2014.

"Light" was originally commissioned by the Hayward Gallery, Southbank Centre, London.

The poetry of Amjad Nasser is the travelogue of an author and his doubles. In his relentless search for the feminine-masculine—in body or form, in truth or myth—and in his examination of wandering, of exile's cities that have become the poet's daily mirrors, Amjad Nasser is always on the hunt for alterity.

It's cliché to think too much of his Bedouin ancestry, his "genetic" predisposition for the peripatetic, his insuppressible urge for travel, dislocation, and translocation. And it is equally incomplete to attribute much of this to anxiety—as if drifting is a treatment plan to attenuate severe boredom in the life of a passerby on this earth and its discontents. Simply perhaps Amjad Nasser was born to become an author whose primary concern is "the history of concealment."

To start with, "Amjad Nasser" is not the name his parents gave to him at birth. When in his early twenties he left Jordan to join the Palestinian revolution in Lebanon as journalist for the cause, he was asked to choose a pen name. He assigned himself an ordinary name, away from any mythic, religious, literary, or national signification, and not a nom de guerre. Yet without Palestine "Amjad Nasser" would not have happened. And without "Amjad Nasser" a life spent searching for doubles would not have begun.

"Preparing for Flight," from his landmark collection of prose poems *Life like a Broken Narrative* (2004), is one of only two poems that mentions the poet's birth name. It's a tender piece for his dying grandmother whose memory was fading fast. When she asks him "Who are you?" he can offer only one answer: "Yahia," the name he no longer lives with or by. The paradox is twofold when considering the name in Arabic means "He Lives." In "Preparing for Flight," after three decades of absence, "Yahia" returns reduced to a presence among the dead or dying. But "Amjad Nasser" is not without its boundaries. At times it, too, approaches apparitional existence. In one of the newer poems, "By Chance as Well," the poet has grown ambivalent about his entire exile, his double life and its catalysts, irony always held in the fist:

Even if you did say that chance was your life's heroine, that she
is the one who delivered you almost whole to a city many before
you had reached, you only captured her with your pen name
whose lack of blood type did not raise anyone's suspicion. . . .

Whether the city is Beirut or London, "Amjad Nasser" managed to become one of the most important writers in Arabic today, a writer with a palpable, traceable body of work and history of movements.

Amjad Nasser was born in 1955 in Mafraq, Jordan. The name of Nasser's birth city means "junction" or "intersection." Historically the roads through it have headed north to Syria, east to Iraq, west to Haifa, and south to Amman. After moving to Amman and catching the fever of the Palestinian resistance, its dreams and perils, he moved on to the cosmopolitan Beirut, to its cafés and civil war and liberation movements. There he published his first two books in 1979 and 1981. Along with hundreds of intellectuals, Arabs and non-Arabs, who had supported the Palestinian cause, he left Beirut after the Israeli invasion of Lebanon in 1982. He spent a few years in Cyprus when that island nation served as transitional center of an Arab culture in exile. There Nasser published his third poetry collection, *Shepherds of Solitude*. Next, in 1987, came London—where he still lives and works, as he always has, in journalism.

In the opening lines of an earlier "Chance," from *The Strangers Arrive* (1990), his first collection after moving to London, Nasser gathers the possibilities of his being into a space-time continuum: "I arrived with the others, / slightly before them, / and after they spread their tools on the ground / to gauge the distances." This is not so much a clever ploy or an offering at the altar of logos. It's more of a nod to the insomniac dream diary of his early exile days. In those poems, especially of the third and fourth collections, one can see the poet struggle to forge new terrain for his art. He wanted to subsume it with the daily details of the world around him. But how to achieve this "while defeat rang in his throat / like the bell around the largest ram"?

What is a poet to do when exile's loneliness takes hold "in a tightly sealed container"? Amjad Nasser resorted to love poems, poems of intense desire. In *Joy to All Who See You* (1994), he shifts dramatically to the bliss of intimacy rather than the desolation of exile. He chants his invocations and is intoxicated:

"Show it to me / just aroused from sleep, / bloated with promise, / dew on its crown, / pomegranate seeds / adorning its ears." Some of Nasser's earlier poems, such as "Shepherds of Solitude" and "Shade Plants," examine the theme of love, mostly of the lost and unrequited variety. But in *Joy to All Who See You* love poems are invigorated by sensibility and passion that alter the poet's diction. In "Invocation for Entering the House," language becomes a vow that "has cracked the shell of its parentheses." Or so the poet hopes. The speaker's covetousness and erotic appetite are explicit, and the process of naming, of finding a new name, begins again, this time in the beloved.

"A Rose of Black Lace" is a tense poem, packed with a history of naming, conscious of reflex. The litany of "white" in the poem means many things, not all of them perceptible. To add to this mystery, Nasser begins the collection with an epigraph from one of Paul Celan's early poems (that other poet with a pseudonym): "White what remains mine / white what I lose." The "white" in Celan's poem is specifically that of white hair. "White" in Nasser's passionate collection seems alarming when juxtaposed to Celan's predetermined tragic weight. Yet, similarly, the white that Nasser seeks to name rebounds to him like sonar waves, in simultaneous possession and dispossession, presence and absence. He alludes to this in "A Dusk Foretold" from the following collection, *Ascent of Breath*: "Lack / with its whiteness / lures you."

Reading the poems from *Joy to All Who See You* and *Ascent of Breath*, one senses that Amjad Nasser was writing himself out of love poems as he was writing himself in them. He tried to contain the beloved in the net of his praise but his efforts proved futile. Quickly the poet realizes his wish to claim his beloved is in vain:

> I didn't own you when I repeated your name, or through the kisses
> that fell from my mouth on the ground you'd walked on. A person
> who passes through your regions may leave his name behind but
> not necessarily a vacancy in your heart. It was you who owned me:
> through an innate weakness in my embryonic days. . . .

To make the act of naming endless is perhaps the beloved's way of delaying the process of possession in order to thwart its possibility. There's a reversal of the narrative of Scheherazade here: "A rose of black lace / at the nexus of thighs / the kiss of the happy king / on the thousandth night." It's the poet who's doing the talking. He has entrapped himself in speaking the insufficiency of his language. As if reaching silence was the only way he might begin to see and hear the unnameable illumination of the beloved.

At the cusp of this excess Nasser's trip to Andalusia returned him to his ongoing meditation on exile. By this point the desire in *Joy to All Who See You* had disseminated throughout his estrangement. In order to exit or temper his language, to transform within it, he had to go through *Ascent of Breath* (1997). The inspiration for this collection is the life of Abu Abdallah Muhammad Al-Saghir, the last Arab prince of Granada, whose ousting in 1492 brought Arab and Muslim presence in Iberia to an end. Remembered by many artists since then (and here Amjad Nasser recalls Washington Irving), Al-Saghir's grief, symbolized as the Moor's last sigh, still evokes a durable emotion in Arabs and non-Arabs alike. Al-Andalus is not only a paradise lost, but also a paradise that, if recoverable, is still doomed with the history of unsustainability. Al-Saghir's legend offers the poet, any poet, a cosmic backdrop on which to illustrate the state of the soul in the no-man's-land that is the human condition and its recurrent cycles. Both of the poems included here from that collection are in the banished prince's voice: "Wisdom has chosen you / for one of her greatest parables."

Al-Saghir's tragedy is also that of a broken lover. The tone in *Ascent of Breath*, especially in the title poem, hearkens back to some of the poems in *Joy to All Who See You*. Amjad Nasser was bidding a version of himself farewell while channeling, rewriting, another's personal history of farewell: "I fell the way a clown falls, happy in his nimbleness. / My lineage would not return me to my status among the tribes." And in another clear and earlier echo of the title poem in *The Strangers Arrive*, the poet ends "Ascent of Breath" by conjuring that arrival-departure spectrum:

> O my lightness
> raise me
> or drop me with a bent shoulder
> to calm the dust erasing my childhood traces
> among the pomegranate trees.
>
> O my lightness
> the stranger has arrived
> with a yesterday or a tomorrow,

the stranger
has arrived
riding his
last
breath.

A quick year after *Ascent of Breath* Amjad Nasser published *Whenever He Saw a Sign* (1998). Short poems abound and haiku breaths replace the extended respirations of longing and desire in the previous two collections. "The Edges of Day" is the centerpiece of this new collection and is a remarkable elegy. The long poem is for a dear artist friend who died in Paris. In it Amjad Nasser's barometer measures the absurd. Satire and sorrow are at ease with the fabular in a scientific age. His capacity to unify the timeless with the times is extraordinary:

Naked I left and shall return with my best clothes.
My mother, hostage to her longing, waits, and mothers
weave a waiting whose cotton has no likeness; and my father,
the failed acrobat, balances cancer with dread on his most robust
vocal cord. My days are up in a city whose men mate
with nursemaids of lightning and feed on inductors.

Once, a utility worker
came and found the electricity
meter disconnected,
didn't understand
how my room was pulsating
with volts!

This brings us to the limelight in which Amjad Nasser's oeuvre bathes, the last poetry collection he published more than twelve years ago, at the young age of forty-nine, before his poetry entered a domain of silence. *Life like a Broken Narrative,* a volume of prose poems, attempts to gather as much of Nasser's stop-and-go existence as possible. As in a family reunion, all the aspects that Nasser had addressed in his previous poetry come together to line up in solidarity and fortify his life in his favor or against it. The poet goes back home to his parents' house, visits people who had a deep impact on him, and travels to sites that impressed him in childhood. His travels are now in plain sight behind him. He meditates on his life in exile where he has discovered the pleasures of domesticity. He confronts his romantic victories and failures. Love poems return in "Something like Anger, like Betrayal." Could that be the same lover of "A Rose of Black Lace"? His language and his naming seem to have come home.

This collage of the various facets of his life shows him as a masterful narrator and shaper of wonderful parallels. His neighbor Mrs. Morrison, a stodgy middle-class English woman, turns out to be much like his own grandmother. Things change: the old radio is tossed in a storage room, left to fend for itself among other discarded objects. Things remain the same: a mysterious ring offers him powers he cannot harness, a mystic appears with an arm that comes off at the socket, and his sisters still keep time in the family household by the different kinds of tea they make.

Shunning his command of the poetic line—between short and long—Amjad Nasser gives himself fully over to the sentence in these poems. Impossible at times to replicate in English, his sentences are sinuous and rangy. Sometimes entire poems are one sentence, other times each paragraph or stanza is a sentence. But the pleasure, both in Arabic and in English, is worth the risk. One can think of only a handful of accomplished writers who have achieved this kind of layered and cumulative familiarity with the sentence.

After all his travels and all these cities, and after having lived in London for nearly thirty years with a command of English that meets his daily requirement and a command of Arabic that reaches far and wide into the history of the world, it's no coincidence that Amjad Nasser chose "Cavafy's Mask" as the closing poem of his *Life like a Broken Narrative*. Constantine Cavafy is that other desiring Arab and inimitable exile. Nothing helped alter the poet's reality in the end, "night after night," "in the same alleys," "without escape / or path." Ithaka, Cairo, London, they are the same.

Yet didn't Amjad Nasser know this since his first collection? He began it in 1979 with an epigraph from Cavafy's "The City." And in the collection's opening poem, "Gates to the Sky, but They Are Narrow," he wrote that "the city had not yet become / a losing bet." He always knew that it would.

"Symmetry repeats / but dimensions vary." That's what the poet tells us in one of his new poems, "Petra: The Concealed Rose." This seems to be the method with which, over twenty-five years and eight poetry collections, he tackled or postponed his inevitable encounter with vanishing, or an idea of vanishing at least. As regards to poetry, Amjad Nasser has almost written himself off the page. His doubles have walked away from the field and he seeks them elsewhere now, mostly in prose. Since Nasser's *Life like a Broken Narrative* appeared, he has published five books, none of them poetry. Four of these titles, the two memoirs and the two travel books, waltz with the notion of mixed genre. In this, too, Amjad Nasser performs his travel and translocation within text itself. The text contains its doubles.

Amjad Nasser continues to dissolve the line between poetry and prose in his new and few uncollected poems. Of those poems, "Petra: The Concealed Rose" is a masterpiece. As travelogue in verse that doubles and doubles back as travel guide, not as epic, it's a poem the likes of which are not many. "Petra: The Concealed Rose" belongs to the world's literary gems. It becomes the ancient place that provides new alterity for the poet. The poem's rich catalog contemplates the masculine and the feminine, the historical and the mythic, the mystical and the erotic, the Arab and the non-Arab, the Bedouin and Johann Burckhardt, the ancient and the contemporary. But this leaves the poet with a single lasting interest. When Amjad Nasser asks "Where is Petra's childhood?" he is also asking about his own and ours. And he is left face-to-face with disappearance once more: "Don't seek me in simile, for all who are like me are not me, and all who resemble me are other than me." Is there a place in which one can lay his selves to rest better than Petra: a name that is dead but not extinct, alive but not living, lived through but not lived in? Is this also simply not childhood, "Only this hand / that returned with a map of scents and signs"?

Whether one thinks of Cavafy, Borges, or Neruda, Machu Picchu or Petra, Sufi exegesis or material discourse, cosmic memory or personal remembrance, Amjad Nasser stands in deep camaraderie with the world. His poetic space, his journey with his nom de plume, evokes other great authors. Yet his travel does not necessarily hide a deep reservoir of tragedy. The poet hums to himself the versions of himself that make a life. He is a man who shares one of his two kidneys with his wife: it is love as literal, unadorned transplant.

A MAP OF SIGNS AND SCENTS

from *Praise for Another Café*, 1979

Gates to the Sky, but They Are Narrow

I

I will not defile my face feigning optimism.
I will spread the plank of my chest for the birds
coming from the desert and the sea, and exhale
a bundle of living smoke. Only then will I start speaking.

II

The heart was stubborn,
a boy with reckless hair
stumbling through night's dilapidated branches.
The city had not yet become
a losing bet.
They shot hot lead between the eyes
of the horse that lost. My cramped fingers
did not obey me and reached for a net that held emptiness
or a corpseless grave.
I touched a hand made of pliable steel.
I didn't fire.

The city was drowning
in the sound of neighing.

III

Where will sadness go,
where will cigarettes go
if the cafés disappear?
The minor poets,
their foam,
their impartial criticism,

and their stories, suitable only
for diaries of wretchedness . . .
Where will you build your fabled kingdom, dear dream?

. . . .

. . . .

Cafés are more rooted here
than fingernails are in fingers.
Where's the harm in this?

IV

The heart is a morsel of rare sponge.
It cannot shield itself from the tremors
rushing at it from all sides.
The city could not raise its keen sword.
Despair was the widest of the sky's narrow gates.

V

I will not defile my face feigning optimism
to please the wife and the seven neighbors.
Sadness, the horse most likely to win,
met me on the road
and offered his dark, veined hand.
I shook it and we laughed together.
The city's night is long
without those celestial bodies
made of phosphate and human flesh.
And though they are pavilions
of bad poetry and impartial criticism
thick with the fog of endless cigarettes,
the cafés are low stones,
rest houses for birds coming
from the desert or the sea.

VI

Amman smells of horses
and the lone shirt hung
in the widow's wardrobe.
Amman smells like tired bodies.
I recall:
> *Was the Arab Bank*
> *close to where the river shrank,*
> *close to dawn's first spark?*
> *Was it that far from my heart?*

They begin to tremble those fingers pointing to the sky.
No . . .
It was a summer whose fires would not go out,
a time of collapse.

VII

In seconds, the scene takes shape:
leather bags of different sizes
bearing different contents,
faces that go long
and cloud up,
features shaped by cramped muscles.
The train heads north or south.
No difference. The long whistle blows
a thin, agitated
thread.
And the scene folds on itself.

Cities more distant than this dream,
may this whistling
never reach you.

KM

from *Climbing the Mountain Since Gilead*, 1981

Song

Blood in schoolbooks,
blood in the first note
of the royal anthem,
blood in the military academies,
blood climbing the minarets,
even on the arc of the crescent moon there's blood.
On the slopes of the seven mountains, blood.
Blood between the trees and their bark,
between our lips and our song of praise.

KM

Grandfather

What is this old man waiting for
now that his friends are coughing comfortably
in spacious graves?
The trees that witnessed his youthful strength
now have withered beards and stooped backs.
His stables, built of holly oak wood,
have crumbled into dust that has dissolved
in water that never stops preaching its sermons.
What is this old man waiting for, old man
whose life cannot be priced,
whose age cannot be measured
by the houses he built or the ones that collapsed,
or the horses that died in regions God made and forgot,
now relieved of his unbearable weight?
His grandchildren escaped work in the wheat fields,
escaped floods and wars.
They settled new regions with women and clans.
They ruined cities with rebellions, and tied laurel wreaths
and bullet belts around their waists and chests.
They took horses and tobacco to regions untouched
except by wild goats' hooves.
They built forts, brought dead soil to life,
and spread throughout the land.

KM

One Flower

Flowers in the hair of a woman
going to a dance.
Music, kisses, and gold rings
surround her body.
Flowers on the balconies facing a blacksmith's shop.
It's a simple evening:
artisans and retired workers,
lovers unemployed by love, and grocers,
the same evening facing all the balconies.
Flowers in the room of the novelist who has a deer fetish,
deer and murdered revolutionaries in the novelist's room.
Flowers, deer, and a novelist in a single room.
Flowers in colorful clay pots.
Roof tiles on houses inhabited
by the acids of happiness.
Flowers and sex and rumpled silk stockings
in the college dorm rooms.
And college girls and wine.
Birth control pills in their apartments,
college boys deep into women and political rallies.
Flowers in the poets' poems,
lice in the poets' hair,
and the poets loaf about without flowers or poems.
A carnation in the old politician's lapel.
The old politician tosses away the flower to protest the war.
The war does not end.
The flowers of the four seasons
are in the garden of the bourgeois divorcée
who every evening drives
along the seashore.

She is looking for a hole
in the wall of man.
Many flowers
and one flower for me,
which
a stranger
tosses
through my window
thinking his old
lover
still
lives
here.

                                        KM

Shoes

Shoes hurt us,
and in order not to go mad
from the plastic and leather that shackle our feet
we forge shapes and colors
and babble about their elegance and sturdy make
when visiting friends or at cafés.
Shoes hurt us,
and we are sad
since in these cities
that are built out of fish bone
we cannot walk
barefoot.

FJ

The Bleating of Copper

Fathers
told us about raids
and deaths avenged,
but they never spoke of martyrs.
The bells of the flock
were everything,
the bleating of copper
that never ceased to ring
and the rivers and oases
that slipped from under
the hooves of their horses at night.
Night and horses—
is this all that history tells?

KM

from *Shepherds of Solitude*, 1986

Exile

Can't you see?
We haven't changed much.
Maybe we haven't changed at all:
the loaded phrases,
the Bedouin accent,
the long embrace,
the questions about family and livestock,
the ringing laugh,
the smell of old wood
(wood stored in stables)
still lingering on our clothes.
Can't you see?
We haven't changed much,
maybe not at all.
We squat and jabber
while jumbled laundry hangs on clotheslines
in our front yards,
beside children covered with grime.
Mint tea in the evening,
lively gossip,
contentment with little,
and obsession with revenge,
the blood thicker than water—
all this
as if we're still in Mafraq or Al-Salt,
in Kerak or Ramtha,
as if we never crossed northern borders
to the big cities
and coastlines

where wars rage
and seas surge.

Here strangers grab each other
by the collar
or fire their guns
from balconies
into each other's clothes.

KM

Drums

We'll go then,
O country
stamped with red wax
and shrouded with oleander,
to your final resting place,
we'll go with tattered banner
and bowed heads,
without zeal
or sorrow, we'll walk
in your funeral
with only one drum rolling:
my heart.

FJ

Bent Branches

I want to purge my soul
of all signs of obedience
and the last clots of forgiveness.
I want to cleanse my face
and wipe off the tribe's features,
cut off the branches of the family tree.
I want to erase poetry's rot
and the futility of remembrance.
I no longer wish for gray, hazy dusks
or to stand under an array of spectral lights.
I want
only
to hear the tremor of the world
beating against my heart's walls,
to see
light
dissolve
in the swamp waters of my eyes.
I want to clear my head
of all that remains of sermons and the good word.
I want to purge my heart
of the rubble of first love, its shards of glass.
I want to clear my eyes
of the moon's tattered nets,
curtains that shutter windows closed.
I want to purge my voice of the acid of song,
of cries wrapped in silver threads.
I want to shake off the bird nests
on my shoulders, those mute morning birds.

I want to cast off from my body
the shirts of war and peace
and wipe away the dust of opposing conquests.
And walk alone,
shut the stable door behind me.

KM

Loneliness

I

At night when walls breathe and concrete clouds spread between fingers and under nostrils; when we search through wrinkled faces and fissured hands; when we pound sound into tightly sealed containers and no echo comes; when we raise our arms and their shadows don't fall; when no one knocks at the door or passes by the window; when we don't hear the creatures crawling in closets or the howling of love in adjacent rooms; when we rush to the drawers but don't find family photos, search for a gun, switchblade, noose, but only find the plaster of walls cracking in total silence; when we search for our names and don't remember them; when, dear God, all this happens at night, in a tightly sealed container, what do we do?

II

It'll be too much for us,
as it was for those before us,
to slap our palms against each other
for loneliness to fall
off the clothes hanger onto the dresser.

III

Loneliness isn't in a whistling
launched from the top balcony; that woman
who said good-bye to her husband in the morning
was found smeared with the blood
of a slit-throat sparrow.

IV

They're the ones who arranged everything and announced the results:

A man is pacing the corridor back and forth
while a moon bulging at the sides hangs down from his neck.

A man is leaning on the evening paper waiting
for a woman who won't come.

A man at the window waves to pedestrians
who proliferate in dust.

A man in front of a woman, while between them
a partition of isolation's oxide.

A man in front of a mirror, tearing at blood vessels
with a kitchen knife.

V

It'll be too much for us,
as it was for those before us,
to slap our palms against each other
for loneliness to fall
off the clothes hanger onto the dresser.

FJ

Fever

A sway and a stoop,
a slight movement in the shoulders,
a throat shaking off drunken butterflies,
a foggy picture of kitchen utensils,
a light perfume wafting from the wood.

The woman's silhouette stands behind glass:
a silent dialogue,
a halfhearted wave pulls the ragged clothes
off the body's branches.

Ten fingers extend to raise ten violins
toward the mouth.
A ringing from an anklet, a trembling leg.
Two marble shoulders support the window.
But somewhere else
someone is playing the violin of suffering,
someone is emitting fever in the shape
of a sorrowful whistling.

KM

Shade Plants

I

Like a woman who's inaugurated her lover with ramifications, like a pepper plant that has returned the masculine scent to the garden, love isn't possible.

The man sneezed, went on between white and black threads, but didn't fall in love, because love, like sleeping in the lights of spaceships, like a peeling equatorial language that ripened on the throne of dotting, isn't possible.

II

And when we passed, they were arguing about love; a woman leaped out of a low window and gave the impression that the war was still raging in the full quarter of the glass.

It was a time when anklets weren't commonly thought of as a possibility for seduction, and we heard, while riding our horses, a weeping that resembled the stamping of coins. We didn't hesitate when the horses' necks shuddered, and we spurred them on, even though morning had reached us and the weeping maintained its high pitch in the books.

A man said, they were three and their fourth was a dog.
Another said, they were four and their fifth was a dog.
A woman who smelled of chamomile said, you'll find water
by the shoulder of the mountain, wash your clothes there and go to bed.

Shortly thereafter, electricity returned and said hello, and love became impossible in the shadow of shade plants that occupied the corners of the room.

FJ

Eleven Planets for Asia

Since you are the enamored with arches and howdahs and extinct
languages of tribes that lean on willows and weep, you leaned
on the palm tree of my soul before princes, eulogies, and the stony
splendor of the thousand nights fell.
One more night and the silver branches will be full
for the horizon that inclines on my shoulder. One more night
and the Qahtanite will wear a sword of spring fuzz and lead the horse
of his desires through marble pillars toward the renaissance of the body.
Seduction leans to the north in this wilderness
that is laurelled with the moon's dew. And the lands—which are in awe
of copper thunder and ram horns painted
with history's fragrant dust—passionately chant: This is Asia!
And since you come from the evening of technology and species
of indigent creatures, you see Pleiades gleam over camel humps, and see
drawn daggers in the fear of wolves glisten like an encounter.
You see temptation's star light up the sealed blackness in a veiled man's face.
And since you come from the steam of rivers that are suitable for boating
and for body parts that are ready for touching, you find in the shadows of two
ebony shoulders the shade of a continent drowning in sand and weapons.

Asia, Asia,
sands, rifle butts, tribes
that slaughter camels which kneel on one-and-a-half knees.
Moons that dangle from the throne's cupola
via hemp ropes and wail in the nights of delirious cities.
Asia, Asia,
regions of mustard and aging falcons and improvisations.
Asia, Asia,
Adam's apple stabbed by thirty prophets
and eleven planets.

No place for freckled sparrows
and tar forests.
No site for high-tech hands
in the handle of a plow pulled by Hammurabi's bull.
Because we write what we don't know
then head to the celebrations of speech.
Asia is words that are born in the mouth
and fields that ascend to the scythe's blade and curve.
Asia! No one's seen her face
except a war that erases its features
then proceeds toward the personal
narrative of ash.
Because war is no longer war,
bullets are carnations that died of yearning,
and marble grows on highlands.
We're in Year One, before Zero.
Asia has undressed, is nude
and has gone to sea:
brides of holly oak,
swamps of wisdom,
hearts of jujube
cooing on the corners of drought.
Pebbles shine
in the jaws of a waterwheel,
children gather manure
to fertilize the continent of bread.

FJ

Shepherds of Solitude

I

Who will describe his transformation
and map with a Bedouin dagger
the parameters of his wisdom?
Who will write about a boy flung by the forces
onto solid concrete
where no dream grows
that is not crowned with defeat?
Who will say that he entered Amman on a spacious,
limpid morning in the year of the great opening,
the year of the earth's fever, and trembled
before a blonde reading the book of disputation?
Who will say that he took off his sandals and washed his hands
with a secret water, that he left his name and coat behind
then pinned the carnation of eternal refusal directly to his chest?
Who will know that on a rainy, low-hung morning
he will look upon things and nothing will reach out to him
except an image of two hazy fingers trembling like waves
in his hands?
Like a man seeking a kiss
or a duel,
he moves on
with a bloody rose in his chest
and a stone in his fist.
Who will know that his mother wept
because he did not wear the woolen sweater she never finished knitting?
Who will know that his father, the old infantry officer,
arched his eyebrows when his letter reached him?
He banished his younger brothers because the letter did not begin:
"Dear Father, dear treasure,

loved beyond measure . . ."
Have you seen him enter cities
and leave
thin
and wet like pigeon feathers,
distracted like a prophet,
lonelier than al-Farazdaq's wolf?*
Sword without a handle,
horse without legs,
a bloody rose in his chest,
a half-moon on his brow.

Man,
son of the dark woman
crowned with silence and gloom,
son of the good father,
there are four lilies shining through the crystals of brotherhood
that surround your picture in a wooden frame.
There are four daggers in sheaths made of mint
ready to slit the sacrificial ram's throat on your doorstep.
The Verse of the Throne throbs at the entrance of the house,
a basil pot, a fish mouth for a charm,
and the lemon tree
crestfallen in the evening
between mother's silence
and father's firm stride
beside the stone path where
a longing leads the old lover
to the scent of her first embrace.

Man,
son of the haggard woman
crowned with silence and gloom,

*Al-Farazdaq (né Hammam ibn Ghalib Abi Firas), ca. 641–ca. 728–730, is an Arab poet famous for his lampoons, especially his poetic exchanges with his rival, the poet Jarir (ca. 650–ca. 728). Al-Farazdaq is considered the best satirist in classical Arab poetry.

son of the good man,
a cloud leans on your sagging shoulders,
and shadows have crawled to where your hand rests.
A wounding rain will fall between
your song and the plains of Moab.
The polestar has taken refuge in your soul's bower,
and your lips bite on a dying thrill.

Man,
son of the woman
crowned with silence and gloom,
son of the good man,
the floral shirt with which you tempted the soldiers' wives
is now worn by a friend who follows in your footsteps.
The young widow, to whom desire's star led you
through night dew and the turmoil of youth,
killed herself in the room with the iron door.
Between her navel and breasts raised like traps
you wrote with henna:

> *Your flame is not in fire*
> *but in the heart.*
> *Give me a lock of your hair*
> *and go.*
> *I did not know love*
> *but I knew how to stand*
> *in the light of the last star*
> *behind a fence made of poplar wood.*
> *Give me a sprig of basil and go.*
> *I'd never known how to kiss*
> *but from my mouth butterflies escaped*
> *and a field song sounded . . .*
> *Give me a shattering kiss and go.*
> *Since the bells that rang*
> *from little lambs' throats,*
> *I have longed for the ringing of the anklet*
> *that gives your left heel*

its golden gleam.
And since childhood,
since the time of dispersal
and my one-eyed sleep,
I have dreamt
of what I am dreaming now.
Give me
your hand
so I can sleep.

II

For a short time he lived in clarity.
Now he is lost among words
and in the fog that grazes on the shoulders' grass.
He stands accused among meanings,
brittle and soggy like a morsel
fit only for a lazy hoopoe,
like a flower that exudes a scent of despair,
like nothing at all.
And on those nights
when the family
brushed white dust off
the stone of sleep
and sought powerful visions,
he bent, then dove into solitude.
He let go of a scream
that swayed in its high loneliness
and fell:
Master, you . . .
He bears the tattoo of his lineage
inherited for eternity to be carried into epochs of fire.
He holds the blade of revenge to the mirror of revelation.
In the midst of rapture he talks
with a woman who lifts her dress above her knees
and treads a river of ringing bells.

In a wilderness that blood cannot reach
until it is greened like death,
where imagination is in drought
and ancient prophecy is in its eternal spring,
and where commandments chew on sticks to clean their teeth,
he flowed like liquid on the road
and hissed with snakes.
He wove a path through the Milky Way
with a thread of goat hair,
befriended a wolf and walked alongside him
on feet of boxthorn.
He let down his hair for a young eagle
who was lost, but found its way to him instead.
Behind the fence of his soul
lions roared, eager for the pounce
and the cracking of bones.
A cage in his chest,
a leap from the horse of his heart,
a cry in his throat
that would slay a bird of prey,
O Master, O . . .

III

Did he know when he sought the foot traces
of the shepherds' wisdom
that the prince, who led a cavalcade of lovers and thieves
and entered the tunnel of heroism, had left nothing in riotous cities
except a crowned darkness and the remains of trumpet squeals?
Did he know that a false prophecy
shot him out of the thicket of brotherhood,
out of his mother's cape
into the mumblings of concrete and lavender grass
piercing the barracks' tin sheets?
Did he know as he wrote the songs of Moab
that Amman would stab his heart

with the copper shrapnel of tribes banished
when the new dams were built?
The city's door was studded with spying eyes,
bodies as tall as cypresses,
hearts made of stone.
They took off their shoes
at the door of love,
kissed the prince's hand
adorned with gold,
and planted the ground with reeds.

IV

He had to begin this beginning
to reach the ends of his wits
like a lost beast with a collapsed heart.
Defeat and despair weighed on him
and he was like a wolf eating
the corpse of another wolf
under a sky
empty
of God.
He had to . . .
He did not reach deep into contentment
or into companionship,
did not go far into the earth,
or far north
where the trees
seek hearths and axes.
He had to begin at this end
and go to this extent
while defeat rang in his throat
like the bell around the largest ram.
He had to
deny his astonishments
and select among them.

He had to duck under the spear of time.
He
had to . . .

What sky is this
that you can't even whistle at,
or quarrel or swap
curses with?

  N
  O
  H
  O
  P
  E

Sky that stifles stone.
No use.
And stone stands firm in the bareness of creation.
Like an eagle in the chapter of rage
he chews on a morsel of annihilation.

V

He seeks you,
not salvation,
the man who went past.
He speaks painfully of loss, then dies.
He searches
among a throng of metals
during an ambush of isolation.
He seeks a description that does not follow what is described
and puts it down without ink.
He seeks a lost beast
to whom he will cry:

 Friend,
 let's live together.

You are a lost prince, dear beast, like me,
seeking an evergreen desert
and shepherds who feed the birds
the meat of their shoulders
to enter
the dominion
of the
seasons.

KM

from *The Strangers Arrive*, 1990

Chance

I

I arrived with the others,
slightly before them,
and after they spread their tools on the ground
to gauge the distances.
The native helpers named the targets,
measured the angles with their expert gaze.
The professionals had the task
of categorizing the facts.
Their assistants' intelligence exceeded prior reports
and this left room for speculation.

II

They settled on street corners.
They built a hangar to receive other escapees.
Among those who arrived,
I too won this bounty by chance.
Since then patience
became
a hard
seed
between
my teeth.

KM

The Strangers Arrive

The strangers arrived from other shores and huddled
in forts that towered above the postal roads.

He thought of boys who ambushed mailmen in alleyways,
forced them to confess the strange sources of their stamps.

He thought of public notaries and scribes
who sat on wooden platforms, sending their minions
to the markets to apprehend farmers and nomads who had lost
their way among the circles of justice and relief.

He thought of bureaucrats whining under ceiling fans.
They sat and spun on swivel chairs as servants plied them
with glittering sugar and ginger ale.
In their files, dams collapsed and villages fell to ruin
as thoughtful tax collectors dozed.

He thought of thieves wearing canvas shoes who robbed
camps abandoned by soldiers who left them to subdue
rebels who disturbed the outlying districts
of a land ruled by a king who was once caught spying
on women who stripped hair from their legs
with lumps of caramelized sugar.

He thought of a prince who survived a massacre of his aides.
When he woke he saw a caravan urging a frightened boy to sing.
The boy told them the tale of a night of concubines
and mirrors that gleamed with shining swords.

He thought of a friend who was murdered on a side street
by thugs who wanted to prove that the morning paper
can deny a man's death, and that a mother's tears in a distant city
are a practice that should altogether be ignored.

He thought of a day scented with mint on which a parade
of blind snails slugged toward their demise at the edge of a jungle.
Women there unfurled their aprons on sofas and fed their children
gruel their neighbors cooked. They held a feast for pilgrims just returned
from performing mysterious rituals in the motherland.

He thought of a general who leaned on his spear for forty years
facing foes who had turned to stone on the plane of his vision.
When they saw birds feeding on his head,
his foes resumed their march on the villages.

He thought of a holy man and his companion,
soon joined by criminals who humiliated
a village and turned its people vile.
When they saw a boat that belonged to orphans, the holy man sank it.
And when his companion stared at him in disbelief,
the holy man answered,

> *Have I*
> *not*
> *told*
> *you*
> *that*
> *you*
> *are not*
> *steadfast*
> *enough*
> *to remain*
> *with*
> *me?**

The strangers who stitched day to night lay
sprawled among torn curtains and food-stained plates.
They helped the natives prolong their insomnia

---

*This encounter in the poem refers to the story of when Moses met Al-Khidr as narrated in sura
Al-Kahf ("The Cave") Quran 18:65–88.

with archives,
machines,
and maps.
They wiped the morning milk staining their lips
and thought of people who smile
at them when they meet,
and who, as soon as they turn their faces,
begin to beat
and beat their animals
with sticks.

KM

The Impending Hour

. . . and when dawn light flared, the princes fought
their desire for sleep and slaughtered goats
from the steepest mountains with golden swords . . .
This commotion continued in a story that unfolded
before witnesses who had hauled vegetables and livestock
to the marketplace.

As if in dream they recounted what they saw:
Roosters eat their cockscombs.
Screams shatter like glass in hallways
and flow like liquid on marble floors.
Dusty horsemen take off soiled helmets in bedchambers
and order servants to speak their native tongue.

A buzzing pierces through cardboard,
pours terror into the seamstresses' hearts.
Birds lure short trees and fasten them to distant waters.
Hunchbacked moons swing like fans
over motionless creatures in the hills.
Women in labor cling to a wayward moon.

Dancers cavort with lovers who had just left
their wives' embraces.
A false ringing sounds from
coins that thieves exchange for tins of tobacco.
Clerks gaze at tombstones seeking legal addresses.
Women show drowsy judges
the whiplash marks on their hips.

Shepherds slaughter a ram before a lover who exaggerates his surprise.
Fishermen with anchors and leather belts
spread enormous nets on the rocks
and toast the pirates of ancient days.

Birds
leave the scene,
taking off from the tops
of the spectators' heads.

And the princes strip off their bloody
coats and put on gilded ones,
their shoulders gleaming in dusk.
They sheathe their elegant swords in the dew
of the tale
and fold them within
the book.

KM

Lines to Joseph

Brother,
my brother,
why did you strike me with the beauty of your eyes,
why did you plague me with false blood
and lead me to seek the wolf's tale,
only to return with your bloodied shirt?

Why did you leave your scent on the shirt
that would leap from the amber of the fields
to land on our father's face?

You were born under the moon of acceptance
and I under the tower of regret.
You dazzled me with your vision—
eleven stars cupped in your hands—
then left me in the grip of sin.

O Brother,
my brother,
why did you strike me with the beauty of your eyes?

KM

The Lion

Lying in wait, in the rough of night, for a virgin, his is the fire harvest owns yet his is the aloneness of urns.

FJ

from *Joy to All Who See You*, 1994

White what remains mine
  white what I lose
      —Paul Celan

Invocation for Entering the House

I

Cross the threshold,
enter
with a throbbing
of light,
this light.
Grieve now for the one holding a long spear
standing at night's gate,
then take him to his loved ones who long for him.

II

Cross the threshold,
with joyous steps.
The promise
has cracked the shell of its parentheses.
And time, that assassin of seasons, now bends its frame.
We grew up, then grew old in a glimpse of your heel.

III

Cross the threshold,
say the Lord's name.
At each glimpse of you a flock of doves takes off
whiter than the sleeper's bed,
and each spark of you
guides a lost moon to its orbit.
With your right hand, stamp a palm of henna
on the arch above the door.

Despite itself, the darkest of dark nights
turns white
when you place a foot on the threshold.

KM

The Scent Reminds

The scent returns,
the same scent
in all that's left behind,
in all that's inhabited
with shadow and aura,
and reminds.

The scent reminds of gifts no one gave,
of beds in rooms drenched in midmorning light,
clothes wilting on clotheslines,
sunrays that shatter on shoulder blades,
the dust of ruins falling on fists,
breaths seeking new paths to the highest air,
the water of bones
spilled on lace,
the scent reminds of loam,
rams aroused by urine's stench,
space explorers taken with the moon's visage,
the color of amber
and lilac
sodden with rain fallen on mud roofs,
and of wheat stored in stables.
The scent reminds of grasses,
of dizziness,
of what's circular and soft,
of the razor's edge,
the scent, the same scent that ambushes on nights
stitched with a hallucinatory thread.

Let the one gazing at the craters
witness the waking of a butterfly.

The scent rises to nostrils,
a damselfly that flits among the columns
and falls on the threshold.
Bring it closer
to the hunter of weakness
among flakes of gold.
Bring it closer
to the fuzz rising from marble skin,
to the stab of myrtle,
to the coronet of a soporific flower
and whatever returns the mouth to its childhood
and releases the tongue
like a snake.

The scent remains
on the hand
on the nose
on lips
in the folds of breasts
on the curtain
on the emboldened air
the same scent.

How wondrous when the day's domain retreats,
when obligations tumble one after another,
desires release the tigers on their shoulders,
let them roam the expanses of abandonment!

KM

A Rose of Black Lace

A pearl on the nose,
a small star of gold
gleams under a straight gaze.
Nomad of cold climes
gloried with freckles,
stay put a bit so the air can reach
the mushroom
under the plow.

        *

My rains are dry, your lips are wet.

        *

Cold penetrates us through our own depths.
We tremble because the mist of your freckles
has fallen on our wounds.
My heart trembles from an old chill.

        *

Night
is a train pulled by tired bulls,
and a woman spreads her whiteness on the stranger.
White this black-hearted night,
white
treacherous
costly
and tall
wearing a pair of black pumps,
white and blonde
guarded by sleepless grass,

grass for the tame beast grazing
the plain.
White
gleaming
pulsing
widespread,
maker of gasps,
foam white,
and death on a pillow made of tremors.
White
with a birthmark,
with marble,
the white of sapphire,
the white of her turn,
white on the edges of mercury,
of hills without paths to climb them,
a hidden white
wrapped in ribbons
dozing in satin,
white indomitable
white tyrannical
white of sleep and regret
white of clouds raining on beds,
cunning white
that sent us out stripped of our inheritance,
white of lies and obedience,
supplication white and the first showers of rain.
Triumphant white
carrying scents and shivers,
sleeping in his linens,
my little master
who does not rise to the music
of my hand's flutes.
A cone of sugar that melts in saliva,
a lover boy proud of his gold and clothes.

Clean
straight-edged
stretched
in the glistening of olive dew,
washed with rains and storm,
sending a scent
of grass cut in the morning,
a snake spiraling into the aroma
while the great eye looks on.

*

She lets clothes witness with awe
how an arrow pierces a bird made of sleeves.
She leaves her scent;
she leaves other breaths behind her breathless,
the fingers on the fold of the shirt,
the sweat from hips
erases night's ink
and radiates fever's musk.

*

With a touch
I release the sample out of the mold,
and with the light of gleaming water
I reach for
the origin
of the scream.

*

A rose of black lace
at the nexus of thighs,
the kiss of the happy king
on the thousandth night
when the snake spotted with dew
slid and began
to guard the herb.

*

Silk at the top,
princes jostle under its knots.
Saliva pours.
They reach the jewel
prostrate
in supplication,
crawling on their elbows.
I hallucinate my love
and hoard every scrap of air.

*

Show it to me
just aroused from sleep,
bloated with promise,
dew on its crown,
pomegranate seeds
adorning its ears.

*

I want
to see
it
out of its
hiding,
pulling
toward it
all the morning
dew.

KM

Invocation

Your hand dozing on your white knee is white,
the ankle that shines in the night of my eyes is white,
your high shoulders are white
and the broad board of your chest is white,
your wayward doves are white
and the meridian between them is white,
your dome is white, your plain white,
the sleep of narcissus flowers between two oval marbles is white,
your thin waist is white
and your bending is white,
your gait is white, its realm white,
your nightgown strewn behind you is white
and your scent in it is white,
your touch is white
and your tiger in bed is white,
your heaving is white
and my white that spills
is white.

KM

The Sun Flung Its Golden Incisors at Me

I

I didn't own you when I repeated your name, or through the kisses that fell from my mouth on the ground you'd walked on. A person who passes through your regions may leave his name behind but not necessarily a vacancy in your heart. It was you who owned me: through an innate weakness in my embryonic days, through the smallest things, things tossed on a chair or by the edge of the bed, I am your prisoner, no, I am your most faithful prisoner to his imprisonment. Not even my tribe's spears or my brothers' multitude could free my hands from a commanding whiteness I had walked towardwith eyes wide open. As if I hadn't been there, my mouth did call you, bless you, roam your domains and return from the deep shadows with the scent of a planet born from the galaxy of dew. The shirt left behind, the sheet stained with the water of resurrection, the lablab that trellised the walls as you roved above me, like a thresher, which a bull eternal in his rotation draws, all this testifies that I have reached what I have reached: a memory that clouds up and rains. Because after you lift your plowing breath off me you become a cloud that has nothing left to give to the desert behind me, the desert that finds me as a bunch of hills in its mirage, whenever we're done making love.

II

Bedouin woman of the cold, my love is what the sun did to me, it flung its golden incisors into my back, and I began to partridge-hop around you, swaying between white and black lines unfalling to grey. I won the three moles that are on the back of your shoulder then lost them on the way home. Your whiteness was immortal as you climbed the stairs, the light flowing out of your dark shadows
over your legs
ankles
soles

as it illuminated
only you.

In this isolating light
in which a passerby walks
without being
visible
I pressed forward with my back
as a fistful of dirt
weighed down my pockets.

FJ

The Lover's Ascent

You were born with this name
so that your memory is retold by rain showers
that fall in silence.

With this name
so that travelers will come to you lonely
and defeated, fatigue on their faces
from nights spent devoted to you.
We return to your hands to drink
from their skill in destruction,
from their defeat of love
whose wound you touch and easily heal.

The wound
of an old
love
stretches
its green
shadows
wide
as a lover's
regret.

Why don't they stop, these hands pushing us into columns
as we strive to reach the luminous fruit
lit with the incandescence of the farthest depth?

Our eyes are white with happiness
as if we are blind, but see you through scent
and read your presence with breath.
Our woman,
we fail to learn the ways of ether
yet when you raise your hand, we raise ours

though no mirror is near.
Your air touches us, wounds us
as we rush toward you, all of us, from every direction,
afraid to be alone.

*

Our table
our oil
our bread
and salt.

*

You are there
and we don't see you.
We know you by your scent and the cup you hold.
Your servant refills it
ignorant of what he touches.
We feel for your traces on the table, lick the taste
you leave behind on surfaces and rims.
Virgins arrive and enviously wipe
the shadows your fingers imprint
on wood.

*

Joy to all who see you,
to whoever places his hand on the stone of your knee,
to whoever dips a finger in your navel
and catches the scent of a secret.
Joy to whoever spreads an arm
around your thin waist,
whoever comes to the stream and drinks his fill.

*

Our woman, ours all,
gracious at day,
alone in transparent night,

you laugh and we fall ill.
You dangle our destinies from your eyelashes
and they fall from your glances
into fever
and captivity.

*

We see you on the edge of the bed
wearing your black stockings,
your hair a rainstorm,
your naked back gleaming,
and we fall into a stupor
though we are not drunk.

Show us your face
so that we look more beautiful in mirrors,
so that we rise above the reeds
and trust our limbs
when called to work,
so that we are comforted.

*

We possess you then lose you,
surround you with branches and spears,
but you trick us
while your hand softly holds ours.

*

You are our woman, ours all,
born with these eyes to seem other than yourself,
leaning in comfort, surrounded by the sound of rustling . . .
You are fruit that strangers split
among themselves. We climb steps
where your air plays with people's heads
and where spears are broken on marble.

Proud among our kin
we are duped by a white magic
gleaming with victory,
by poppy smoke streaming from
your sweet seam.

*

Did we catch the scent of apple as we ascended?
Did we see Bedouins bearing short swords
cutting a path through the trees?
Did we hear slaves being freed
with the sound of trumpets?
Did we see lovers guiding thieves to a treasure?
Did we win you, deservedly
white
and unharmed,
bearing the joy of those returning
to warm beds in their homes
after a cold, mountainous climb?

*

You,
your name,
the ring of your voice
your kiss
your saliva
your summit and plain
your succulent twigs
your bee and honey
your humility
the she-lion in you
your mercy
the taste of your salt
your nest
your roc egg

your step
your foot
your toes
your sandals
your precious stone
your marble
the board of your shoulders
your navel
the eye of your navel
your dove
your stream
the trickle of your dew
your slumber
the scent of your sleep
your dreams
your brassieres
your trousers
the incense of your limbs
your lightning
your thunder
your prayer for rain
your rain
the scent of the earth after you
your moss
the instinct of flight in the wings of your sparrow hawk
your to-and-fro
your isthmus
the heavily armed pain poised on the fringe of your kingdom
your isthmus again
your captives and freed men tossed from your highest tower,
kerchiefs and souvenirs of them—
the night dark beaten by your whiteness
empties its rooms to house guests in its wound—
tattoos from your rituals
the heaven of your heaven
the hell of your hell

that no one tastes
unless longing had planted a palm inside him
and it bore fruit
that he was the first to taste . . .
no one
except for he who plucks the gem of confession
from your mouth to his,
except the one who forgets himself
and is recalled by your breath
your cold
your fire
your
sal-
va-
tion

KM

from *Ascent of Breath*, 1997

A Dusk Foretold

A crowd of his former subjects witnessed his embarkation. As the sails were unfurled and swelled to the breeze, and the vessel bearing Boabdil parted from the land, the spectators would fain have given him a farewell cheering; but the humbled state of their once proud sovereign forced itself upon their minds, and the ominous surname of his youth rose involuntarily to their tongues: "Farewell, Boabdil! Allah preserve thee, 'El Zogoybi!'" burst spontaneously from their lips. The unlucky appellation sank into the heart of the expatriated monarch, and tears dimmed his eyes as the snowy summits of the mountains of Granada gradually faded from his view.
—Washington Irving, *A Chronicle of the Conquest of Granada*

I

Under the ruling star
I let my childhood linger on the outskirts of eternity
while fates were being written down.
New arrivals sought no cause for my hardship. They reasoned
the Events by whatever came to mind,
and let forgiveness be the prerogative of eroded memory alone.

The chanters left with their praises,
the virgins with their rustling,
the retainers with whatever they could carry,
and the birds
tired of migration and the hunt
sought God's protectorate.
But what
shelter
awaits me?

No victor
today
except
the one
who sleeps
with his
talons
intact.

II

Archipelagos of cancer,
weeds of demise,
as if the conquerors launched
your life
with stabs that never heal.
You are not dead.
Wisdom has chosen you
for one of her greatest parables.
That is why you have remained
the life of the hand that waved farewell,
the fist that locked the key
buried
in its flesh.

Watcher of wind currents,
gazer at patient soil,
prince awaiting the diamond stab,
refugee of down that fled the body young,
breather of the proverbial exhale.

You stood between what is owed you and what you owe
as the clock announced the hour
in the fortress tower.
Lack
with its whiteness
lures you,

prophecy
has claimed
her full share.

As for those who came from the meadows and plains,
they took their siestas in the shades of their wives
who swept away evil spirits with fans made of roc feathers.

Ancestors sleep high on the beds of eternity.
Sourness
rises.

The beast spreads the realms before you with her horns.

Banishment
undeniable
on the roads,
in the congealed air.
Destinies entrust their affairs
to a dusk foretold.

A droning
takes the throne.

The hands that calmed the mountains' surge
are now calming exhales that shoot out like flames
in houses where baptismal oil is stored.
Grace seeks your pardon.
The holy verses will not sound out again to make the date palms bow.
The brothers behind the borders are a faraway dream.
The strangers who danced on the shoulders of night
will not raise their voices under the windows of Albaicín.*
The moon wanes to a sliver of itself.
Your name is a sign that eyes eschew.
The rhymes that turned drops of dew
into globes in virgin laps
are silent in their books.

*A neighborhood in Granada, Spain.

Cotton now blossoms out of ears and navels.
The old maids are flitting about groping at the scent
of an old masculinity in priestly robes.
In the dry wadis
measles spawns.

You heard endless calls:
the grunting of horses under heavy saddles,
the whistling of spurs,
the rumblings of elders,
the wailing of mothers for their faraway sons.
The clamor of crowds caught between earth and sky.

For a long time
you heard the creaking of memory
and the hissing of the wind through desire's reeds.

III

Master of this apocalyptic dusk,
I saw in the star that nursed your steps
your silhouette struggling in the wilderness.
You were drying the blood spilled in the hall of the two sisters*,
cleaning the door handles,
wiping dust off languid panegyrics inscribed on the walls,
sunning the sheets,
drenching the bed of deflowering in incense smoke,
preparing the table,
pacing with feet lost in reverie
on the marble of memory.
There was nothing for you to do
but to praise the jutting mountains
fated to surrender their stags.
You praised the thick air
and exaggerated the height of the trees,

*A hall in the Alhambra palace in Granada.

you praised the melons of your region,
the waters of your springs
that you offered to raucous guests who hoisted
a bloody horizon before your eyes.

The
defeated
are set
to leave.
Laughter
in the balconies
of dusk
rattles
the jaws
of shapely
women.

IV

You told your vision to no one:
the pirates of sleep came at you one by one
and crowned you king in the affairs of night.
You have roamed cities accompanied
by barbarians and Mudejars,*
witnessed kingdoms buckling
under the wings of forgetfulness,
princesses shedding their gold
falling from the highest desires.
A call instructed you,
"How we rotate days among the living,"
so you gave thanks to mysterious brothers who
filled your cup and overwhelmed you with shifting images,
and you gave thanks to magicians

*Mudejar refers to non-Arab Muslim converts of Andalusia who lived under Christian rule
before and during the Christian reconquest of Spain. The Arabic origin of the word "Mudejar" is
mudajan, which means "domesticated" or "hybrid."

seeking to subdue insomnia
while sealing the cracks in the night
with the wax of wakefulness.

With huge hands they guarded your last sigh
and with leopard-like shapes they awaited the refugees.
The sign
of the past
belongs
to the ferocity
of dusk.
You heard silhouettes narrate your ancestors' lives
to immigrants who chronicle the habits of anxiety
and who write the book of forces
that will never reconcile.

With the hands that surrendered sword and key
you held a flute and began to stab at the ghosts
that multiply in your sleep.
They are your lowly cousins
who have settled with women who sway
between hovels and cages in the dregs of night.
They settled among conquerors who silenced the tribes,
gave them a lineage in the hinterlands,
and forced them to change their names.

KM

Ascent of Breath

I

Neither the spears of the mighty, nor the knives of dwarves
but
your hand,
rather
the fingers of your hand;
no,
your breath
tearing furrows through eternal air,
leaving them seeded with pain carried from tooth to tongue.
I hear them beyond the incense
of poppy, luring the idols of my life,
spreading their palms at the doorstep.
I climb their path, hoisting my confusion as a flag
of surrender to the gales.

II

Not with sword
or diamonds,
but with breath,
he or she
tempted me
away from the summit of my alertness,
tempted me,
I whose back was
supported by the hardiness of my lineage and my invocations.

> All of night was left to me . . .
> insomnia followed by air
> stabbed with moaning.

I fell the way a clown falls, happy in his nimbleness.
My lineage would not return me to my status among the tribes
and my eyes could not waver from the abyss
that lured me with its bells.
Breaths
slid off
their veils,
the hard
air
pulled me toward it,
my right
to rule the realms
waved
its alarm.

III

Like a captive jolted awake
by the turmoil of a startled night
I heard the sound of steps
repeating the small breaths
of rustling fabric.
A silhouette of plumes touched me and I saw your apparition
pouring light on the dark side,
and promising an endless night,
sprinkling its signs
on whomever catastrophe chooses among the duped.
I took off all my earthly implements and said, "I am now light."
Through the boughs I glimpsed traces of your bare feet passing
on the grass, not with my eyes but with my heart's tremors.
I marched on into the land seeking you. I refused
the trackers' wisdom and sought your presence.

IV

On the hill of regret
I denied my birth star
and shed the skill that distinguished me from my peers.
Among the wide shoulders going past
I was the figure bent beneath lightning.
I turned to slopes that silently received the summits' sermons.
Then below a deaf sky I heard the elements splitting apart
at the height of their abandonment.
I came upon hills being born of the mountains' amnesia
and tattooed spirits floating by the horseshoe of midday heat.
I passed boxthorn spreading aimlessly along the paths
and I turned to my brother.
With what strength I mustered I grabbed a fistful from the soil
that harbored seeds of poison and elixir.
Crowds gathered and the dust raised a veil between us.
They returned with spoils of nothingness.
I resorted to a mountain hoping to snatch
a share of what could be seen.

V

Did I see, or was it what fever projected?
Longings waved their lanterns
at people crossing the dark nights of their souls,
who would never lie again in their beds.
I saw forgiveness sheltering brigands who fled the remains of their names.
I saw brotherhood spread between two giants who horrified the realms,
clouds shade an orphan abandoned by kin,
and the treasure guarded by seven ghosts reveal itself.

On that loose evening,
a dying hope held by your captive
recouped its vigor
when your hand

rose
to touch
my hand
and I began to see.

VI

"The heart cannot belie what it sees,"

nor the eye that I graced with forgiveness
and let guard the shadows of those who passed,
nor the hand that brought to me news of my lower limbs;
nor the smell of cardamom that accompanied me
            (wherever I went I gave away a secret
                that
                I knew
                less than anyone),
nor my breath that gave you your body
and that climbed slowly from my soles to my scalp
and almost abandoned me when your heaven began to loom.

Not a single drop of a daisy's blood has ever lied.
    It fell
    and conjured
    a dusk
    that will never
    heal.

VII

. . . But
why won't this glass
and that smoke
release me from the grip of insomnia?
Why do I
not drift away
or waken

as though I had not seen
or heard
or touched
or inhaled your breath
upon my hands?

VIII

It's not the magi's star
or fire lit by my kin tonight
that burns
and captures,
but
your silhouette
passing
between two summits,
or perhaps your breaths
luring promises
that do not live or die,
or my regret
hurling balls of flame
into the vastness of the night
to measure the depth
of the abyss.

IX

Lighter than a hope on a mountain of despair,
like a feather that flees the quagmire of wing,
and heavier than me in the wind's palm—
my soul
is inclined to suffer.
And like my thirsty lips at the edge of the stream,
my hands
set their traps
and return empty.

X

I am crowned with lightness.
My throne is in the air
held by tormented breath.
My lightness left no trace of me on the ground,
but it did not raise me to you.
O my lightness
raise me
or drop me with a bent shoulder
to calm the dust erasing my childhood traces
among the pomegranate trees.

O my lightness
the stranger has arrived
with a yesterday or a tomorrow,
the stranger
has arrived
riding his
last
breath.

KM

from *Whenever He Saw a Sign*, 1998

Meritocracy

For whom,
if not for those who subjugate the nights
while leaning on star and flute,
does silk flutter black in abandonment's beds?

For whom, if not for those who walk lightly on earth,
does reed puncture insomnia's breath?

FJ

Haiku Breaths

I

The smell that emanated from primogeniture's valley
adorned me with a sash.

I gave out orders.

II

Your healing breath
touched the ailing air, cured it;

the same breath emaciated me.

III

One hand near God,
in the other the staff,

a kingdom, a gasp
and a thread of pain.

IV

My fearful hand saw all,
hushed its memory of sliding over
the universe's roundness.

My reckless breaths
spread the fire.

V

It isn't: what gestured to those
who walked playfully in its path?
It's: whose breath ghosted me?

VI

Air's indebted to breath,
love isn't to my heart.

VII

Breaths plow then sow
my body:

memory of a hand's miracle
touching the wing of a bird of paradise.

VIII

Under your lit-up breaths
night rests
from the work of darkness.

IX

Laureled with your breath
you grew me
but condemned my harvest.

X

Are they your breaths
or a cloud whose rain is for another?

XI

Your breath captured me,
promoted me by levels
ahead of those standing in line.

XII

Neither before
nor after your breath
was.

XIII

I don't deny
the face of plethora,

your breaths issue
creation's citadels.

XIV

Ah, this fragrance,
your breath surely must have
strolled about here.

FJ

A Mark

No, it's not the bluish hickey on your upper lip
that would guide the guards to me, but the moaning
of the Sumerian lute under your clothes.

FJ

Alexander's Gold

I saw me in his company riding on horses
that were wiped out by night and churned with all that jangle.
Some of us leaned down, grabbed fistfuls of something
while others didn't (they were asleep or lacked incentive).
Then Alexander the Great told us: *He who takes will regret*
and he who doesn't will regret.
I was next to him, my shoulder almost touching his,
I stood like a statue in the aura of his upright torso
and I neither leaned nor bent.

In the morning we found gold dust on sparkling hooves.

FJ

Kismet

Between two swordsmen my share is split air.

FJ

Appearance

Signs appear to successors;
they lead the blind to what the blind's hands saw,
and grant the frivolous the dividend of wakefulness.

FJ

Father's Sleep

I want to sleep the way my father sleeps,
on his right side,
his arm his pillow, looking with eyes
that have surpassed love and anger
toward passersby
whose shadows are imprisoned
by their torches
and who, along with their trumpets,
the clamor of their camels,
and the smell of their livestock,
are swallowed whole by the night.
Like him,
at the same age,
in the same posture,
with the same yarrow
scent on his skin,
the same steady gaze into the hollow night
that sees and erases what it sees,
I want to sleep.

FJ

The Edges of Day

Because I've never survived a hope without succumbing to another, and
because whenever a mask smiled to me I took it as my confidant, I died,
though not as one who walks gaily among his vigilant friends dies, but as
one who has died a lot, often, so that when death came laughing in its green
plume and drooped my eyes over the gentle light of the valley, I didn't believe
it. I used to think death was a clamor, "a great scream that deposits all that
we've surrendered to, grows rich and abandons us"; not a mere dozing off in
an arid bed
a lonely bed
in the white nakedness.

There are those who die of despair and I died because hope
continued to hop around me, and hope, that hunter of feeble souls,
will guide you to the water springs and bring you back thirsty,
plays with you a game of paper scissors rock.

I did not know
hope had
snuffed out so
many lives.

I have died a lot and persisted to drag myself
under the long arm of promises,
and all who know me know how death becomes a dream
for which the most vicious nights ornament their beds,
incense their sheets,
call to it by the sweetest names
and it doesn't come.

Death isn't easy to seduce over a glass of wine,
and you can't easily toss to it a moon

in whose light lovers have wasted their fortunes of tears.
For whoever sees death's hands as I have
knows how difficult it is for the absentee
to return to drink from his mother's palms.
No one returns as he left
and water has no memory
that preserves the faces of the absent,
and no one dies when he wants.

Don't believe the suicides who throw themselves in rivers
or from the tops of buildings that are packed with the sleeping;,
it was another thing, beside their fates, that had slunk its strand of hair
out of night's dough
and let its curtains down over them.
I tried everything the others did.
But the one who toys with the hours
and feeds scorpions the sugar of absentmindedness
put nothing in my hand.

Once, I swallowed a sleeping pill,
ate berries ad nauseam,
then threw myself across the railroad tracks.
The hum shook my body from the right
jugular to the left
and I aimed my fist toward my heart,
which was hanging by a thread
in the core's emptiness
before I sprang up with all my might,
but nothing fell from the bough
that was dangling by the day's edge;
only leaves yellowed and mummified
in the long autumn of hope.

II

And when I tired from dragging myself among you I slept.
Then I saw a passerby who resembled me.

He was leaning to one side and hoofing it on a slow afternoon.
I tried to discern his features but couldn't,
and each time I tried I kept sinking in some puffy wool;
I heard mutterings and retreating footsteps,
the world got cloudier in my face, beacons
over some mysterious citadels went out,
and buckets were raised from wells whose waters had dwindled;
I heard the creak of pulleys and pulled ropes
and the knocking of empty buckets,
raucousness
movements
shouts
that were
van-
ish-
ing.

I must have died.
Or how else could I have seen all this through my sutured lids
and remained still in the cotton mountain I had slipped into?
My mouth was completely dry, my throat
a Styrofoam box, and what I thought was my voice
was an echo reverberating in a dry riverbed;
what need have I, at any rate, for speech where my parents dwell.
Suffice it to shake my hands free from what I despised
and had rotted my blood,
or
from what I crawled
on all fours
to make my offerings to.

I am now without a name to be called by,
I left him to pick up his own load;
in the partition of water and dirt
shadow does not ask about its roots.

So let the one who toys with the hours and raises scorpions under sturdy towers, let him place his biggest scorpion in the vineyard; the wind has frozen in the flute's reed, and the feather that was falling off the bird of mortality has arrived. I am so touched. I thank you so much for sending me off to my parents in my striped suit and lilac shirt. And I would have squeezed your hands if I'd known what it felt like to touch the hands of the dead.

III

Naked I left and shall return with my best clothes.
My mother, hostage to her longing, waits, and mothers
weave a waiting whose cotton has no likeness; and my father,
the failed acrobat, balances cancer with dread on his most robust
vocal cord. My days are up in a city whose men mate
with nursemaids of lightning and feed on inductors.

Once, a utility worker
came and found the electricity
meter disconnected,
didn't understand
how my room was pulsating
with volts!

I did love and did exit from the other side with more
than one rib
missing; love's claws are not shorter than hope's.

Just ask my heart, which I left
boisterous as a slave freed from the stranglehold of the night
on a road that loved others more,
even when I ripped for its sake
a vein.

I left no railroad fence I didn't jump,
or a street my feet didn't store in their memory,
I wrote stories about love and madness
that my demanding friends didn't like,
because I wasn't concerned with craft as I was
with classifying the levels of deception.

I have nothing to do here or anywhere else,
that's why I leave to you my books, the fires of harvest
in my paintings on my room's walls,
and the promised days that never came,
so give them away to a passerby
who leans to one side between two starless nights.

Autumn is a perfect season to bid Paris farewell.

Dice is falling heavily on nacreous backgammon squares.

Sleepwalkers are returning to their beds.

The mighty are free from grating their teeth.

The sun of serum bags inundates the hospital,
while metaphorical friends are outside smoking
with a boredom their frowning faces cannot hide;
or are they pecking the ground with the tips of their shoes?

There are wolves that don't see with the naked eye,
they are silently squatting behind turns
and on street corners.
And there are those who hear what you cannot hear.

But life
is hope's
slack
saddle
on the back of an indomitable horse,
it venerates its promises,
it gives
and takes
from the bushels
of wind.

FJ

The poem is in memory of Jamil Hatmel.
The quote in the opening stanza borrows from Rainer Maria Rilke.

from *Life like a Broken Narrative*, 2004

The House after Her Death

Nothing has changed after my mother's death.
She is still young in her portraits, my four sisters still intent on keeping
                              the day tied to
her three stalwart rituals: coffee in the morning, ginger tea at midday, and in the
                              evening mint.
At my family's home you do not need a watch.
Aroma will tell you the sun's place in the sky.

Nothing has changed in that house since my mother's death.
My sisters' hands keep busy tidying up the rooms, their five
                              brothers left for distant rooms
where their souls never rest,
for they no longer sleep on mattresses spread on the floor,
or shiver like addicts waiting for their morning tea and
                              bread.

After my mother's death, nothing has changed in the house.
When we look at Kawthar, our oldest sister, intent on keeping
                              even small things whole,
we begin to sense that our mother hadn't left the house (which she built, sigh
    by sigh),
in a white coffin, her body consumed
by cancer, to a cemetery meant to hold the first of the family's dead.

Nothing has changed after my mother's death:
the day with its three levels of latitude,
the tidy rooms awaiting absent sons,
my father's endless marathon between ablutions
                              and the mosque,
and the everlasting nostalgia for the happy days when we were poor.

Everything is still the same
except for that hand that turned the dust green.

KM

Old Radio

To revisit what had once enthralled me, I looked through the storage room (home of things that neither die nor live) for the books that led me to flee the country. That's where I found it: the old radio, a Philips, with its green eye that shone through my father's sleepless nights.

It stood silent, tattered, stripped of its rank as the most important member of the household.

The fine mesh that had poured out emotions, intrigues, and lies is broken. The thick black leather cracked. The old stations (London, Washington, Berlin, Moscow, Tiranë) that stirred peoples and trouble in the East with long harangues stand quiet as gravestones covered in dust.

My father, a tank officer, warned me never to move the needle too fast, fearing I'd set it loose from its fixed orbit. It stood frozen at Radio Damascus, which the family tuned to only during Ramadan to hear the child-voice of Sheikh Tawfiq al-Munjid reciting the Quran.

. . . .

I did not find my secret books. My family probably got rid of them soon after I left. And they were right, for who in Mafraq has any need for *The German Ideology* or *What Is to Be Done?* I found my stifled adolescence there when I was stuck and barely living on rapacious daydreams. The Babylonian sounds that rose and spread reclaimed a life lived only in songs.

KM

Seven Bridges

To my brother Ahmad

When we used to stop at Seven Bridges to look at the gravel-covered valley that has no name (where there is no water, there is no name), we did not know that one day I would find my way to the London Bridge and you to the Brooklyn one.

No one who knew Seven Bridges (the miracle of Al-Zarqa' suspended in ellipses of dust) had ever heard of those two bridges or thought there were bridges more awesome than this one with its seven arches the Ottomans built to lay the Hejaz railroad in the last gasp of their janissary reign.

Gusts of wind pumped under it.
Birds of prey made their nests
    in its crevices.
Women placed charms for their husbands
    between its stones.
Night had assigned it
    to be the keeper of its dark.

Remember how we used to throw coins
and they rusted before hitting the ground,
how we threw a shirt the wind tore in two,
a green branch that instantly turned into charcoal.

But far away in the cold country of England that now implores the rain god to return, there was a bridge (immortalized by an American-born English poet named Eliot) that joined London's two muddy riverbanks. Sleepwalkers crossed it to castles of money, and many suicides bowed their heads before it and threw themselves away. On the other shore of the Atlantic (where Bedouin intuition is useless) stood a more impressive bridge called the Brooklyn Bridge. All the tribes of Jordan can cross it without loosening even one of its screws.

Seven Bridges. My father threatened (in your presence perhaps) to throw
me off if I did not stop smoking and stealing from neighboring orchards, or
chasing after girls then entering our house by climbing over the stone fence
rather than through the front door. My heart fell and did not reach bottom
when he pressed his big hand on the nape of my neck, showing me how far
down the ground was. All the bridges I have seen since have not shortened
that distance from my memory.

It was not the height,
or the gravel floor,
or the grave of Umm Youssef Saleem,
the first of our dead on the other hill,
but the three Ottoman shell cases
I found with my Jina'ah* street gang,
filled with gold Majeedi* coins (according to me)
and filled with spoiled gunpowder (according to the police) . . .

Twenty years after a mythical flight, while eyes that trapped blue flies watched,
I sat on the edge of Seven Bridges and was afraid
to dangle my feet and reveal the distance
between my memory and the ground below.

KM

*Jina'ah is a poor section of the city of Al-Zarqa' in Jordan.
*Majeedi coins are an Ottoman currency that was widely used in the Middle East.

Souvenir

The bullet he shot out of his father's (military-issue) pistol, while playing under an arc of heat and boredom, and that almost killed his younger brother, lodging itself in the middle drawer of the family's first wardrobe, that same bullet was left there (probably deliberately) as a souvenir of the family's eldest who left, vowing never to return.

KM

The Ring from Al-Qayrawan

I

From the very moment I saw this ring in the hand of the poet Saadi Youssef, I was captivated by it.

On that night at Salutation Pub I tried to avoid looking at it, but could not. Saadi must have noticed my fidgeting and that my torso was leaning toward his right hand where the ring was perhaps spewing its fumes through the crack in its crown. I told Saadi that I admired his ring, and he took it off and gave it to me, mumbling something like "what the old pass on to the young." It is difficult sometimes to ascertain exactly what Saadi says, especially when he, for some reason, begins to take the shape of the porcupine of his famous poem.

But this is not the beginning or the end of this ring's story. It had belonged to a Sufi from Qayrawan who had nothing else of value when he died. Perhaps it is the ring of sainthood. The Sufi passed it on to his son who followed in his father's footsteps until he heard Saadi recite his poetry one night in Qayrawan. He especially loved a poem titled "The Ancestors," and to express his admiration to the poet he offered his only valuable possession to Saadi. The poet, famous for his seven stutters, stood confused, unsure of what to do with a snub-nosed silver ring that had a crack on its crown.

II

A year after acquiring the ring I found myself in Southall, the West London fortress of South Asians in England, to expose my senses to the aromas of the East so that they remain alert and so that I do not end up buried by mistake in Greenford Cemetery,* for example. That's when I went into a jewelry shop and asked for the ring to be repaired.

The Indian jeweler asked me if I was sure that I wanted to weld the crack on the ring and I answered affirmatively.

He welded it as much as he could.

*A cemetery in southwest London.

Soon the ring became too tight for my right ring finger, so I switched it to my left where it was too wide and kept slipping off. The shape of the ring changed; it was no longer snub-nosed. The etchings that I thought were calligraphy disappeared. I would give up all of my poetry to know what those etchings said. Were they a riddle that I had failed to answer? Or a message that I had never bothered to read?

I began to wake up in the morning without the normal urges that pricked me like lightning, those expectations and humming, those foolish promises I made to myself. All of a sudden my hair began to gray, but I had no sign of wisdom to show for it, none of that impressive silence, or the renouncement of the rat race for status and fame.

I realized too late
that I had committed a grave violation.
Alas, if only I could know what it was!

KM

Suhrawardi's Handkerchief

If this story had travelled the predatory field of Borges's hawkish ears, he would have snatched it at once and threaded it into his priceless string of prey, beginning with his two kings and their two labyrinths, all the way through the burning of Alexandria's library, which he attributes, without evidence, to Omar ibn al-Khattab, since Borges believed all books hail from one common ancestral book.

I don't know how or when this booklet, branded with "Diwan of Imam Shihab ad-Din Suhrawardi," reached me, but it seemed that since I first saw it in my office, a serious publishing error had occurred, though it wasn't until I opened the booklet that I smelled dry blood, then immediately saw an amputated hand start to hemorrhage, then the hand appeared to turn into a handkerchief that a sudden wind took into flight.

I had hardly cared about Suhrawardi, though whenever I uttered his name a friend of mine, whose suicide didn't surprise me later on, would add "The Murdered." I had hardly cared until I was in Qayrawan, in my room at the Continental Hotel listening to a few of Suhrawardi's verses sung by a Syrian singer who was strumming, in the complete hollow depths, some invisible strings with wounded fingers.

Suhrawardi snuck into me and I became lighter than a feather of a spent bird as it returned home on its last breath, for he must have stumbled on something within me, or why else would I have persisted to repeat to myself for days his verse: "Forever, the souls yearn for you"?

Perhaps it was the consequence of divulgence that drew me to the poem I had not heard of before, and how could a singer with a strand of hair dangling by each of his temples know the poem while I, the poet concerned with the history of concealment, didn't.

But without digression from the bend of stories that maneuver the night, I will tell you, with the voice of one whose wily mask is blindness, the story of

Suhrawardi and the Turkman shepherd, as I hunt it out of the aforementioned booklet, without attributing any of the story to myself as I did with "Alexander's Gold," which originally was no more than a story my grandmother Thannieh Dakheel had told me during my childhood that gathered fragments of chatter in the midst of receiving rebuke and blessed kicks that seemed an absolute right of those who were older than me to give to me:

"We were a group in Suhrawardi's company plodding along near Qabun on the outskirts of Damascus, swaying with hunger, when we saw a flock of sheep herded by a Turkman (he was most likely a Turkman, we could tell by his dress and his terse words with which he scolded his flock), and I asked Suhrawardi for some money to buy a sheep to slaughter and cook (but don't ask me how our internal tigers crouched ready to suck marrow while we were in the company of such a man whose sustenance is one date and a piece of bread?), so Suhrawardi pulled out ten dirhams and said, 'That's all I've got, see what you can do with it.'

"I bought one sheep from the Turkman whose friend thought I'd gotten off easy with too good a deal, and he chased after me and said, 'Give this sheep back and take a smaller one,' but I paid him no attention and caught up with the group only to find Suhrawardi walking without touching the ground.

"Then the shepherd caught up to us, encouraged by his friend's audacity, and asked me to exchange my sheep for a smaller one, and I refused, still the Turkman kept circling me with mutterings that doubtless were muffled curses, and I kept on ignoring him until Suhrawardi told me, 'You go on and let me take care of him," and then suddenly the shepherd started to block Suhrawardi's path wherever the Imam turned, and when the shepherd got no response from Suhrawardi, he grabbed the Imam by his arm, and it came off right at the socket.

"Shocked, as he held in his hand Suhrawardi's jerking and bleeding severed arm, the Turkman dropped it and ran away, and Suhrawardi bent down, picked his arm up, and headed toward us as the air stiffened in our throats, but when he reached us the only thing his hand held was his red handkerchief."

FJ

A Postponed Poem for New York

I

Before what happened happened,
I mean, before the towers became a stairway to the day
of reckoning, and the world split into two
camps, water and sand,
I used to wish that I'd be among the poets
who would curse New York.

The poem was almost ready in my mind.
To write a poem about the jungle of asphalt and concrete
has become a tradition since Lorca
(inspired by Whitman probably, not Gibran)
had anchored the first rule for the poets
who would aim their pointed poem at the Big Apple,
the sex and money cobra,
the Babylon of our time.

It's not necessary that poets throw their explosive
cigarette butts in the Hudson mud,
or swagger drunk on the cheapest liquor
on the Brooklyn Bridge, or listen to jazz howl
in Harlem's glistening knife-dappled night,
or know that the Statue of Liberty with a flame
that can no longer illuminate a beetle's wing
was, originally, destined to the Suez Canal
but when the Egyptian state went bankrupt
to the cadence of *Aida*'s opera
the new rising power, beyond the ocean the Arabs
had pessimistically called the Sea of Darkness,
purchased it. And it doesn't matter

if the poets take the subway with owl eyes
that guard their backs, or if they don't take the subway.
Because he ain't no poet
who doesn't try his luck with New York,
to describe it, defame it, threaten it
with a destiny like Sodom's, even if he has not seen
cruelty's dice, the black tears of colored folks,
the muddy feathers of gray pigeons that are good
for anything except as symbol for a peace
that pours from New York's stony lid.

II

I've never been to America.
I knew it as others do
through movies, dreams, and wars
that gave birth in us—we whose trunks bend
under the weight of its metal ruckus
over the irrigation wheels
of blood and drought—
to two original emotions: love and hate.
And when I once found myself
in the land of maples, I didn't answer the call
of Ahmad, my brother,
who was constantly snatched by the urging
of gold and dust from the east coast to the west coast
until he ended up fighting for survival
behind the metal bars of a gas station
where his buddy was shot dead with one bullet.
I was afraid that my fleeting passage
through Upper Manhattan
would ruin my ferocious poem that cooks
on my slow fires
of acrimony.

. . . .

But since what happened happened,
I mean after September 11 in the year of two
false prophets and their satanic verses,
when humankind discovered,
with sudden metaphysical distress,
that our human hands, which we have long trained
to fly in order

to alight us on the face of abundance, these hands,
when the towers exploded, were not wings
but two sledgehammers that plummeted
us to the ground. Since then
I've been unable to write this poem.
That's how New York will escape,
for the time being at least,
from another invective poem about its vertical vanity.

. . . .

That's a predictable parting blow.
I'd like to suggest
another ending for the poem:
those who flew into the abyss of Resurrection
full of belief that they indeed did possess wings,
if they should ever know
why what happened happened,
think, New York, of the circular time of proverbs,
of blood and heroin dripping from graffiti,
of poisonous mushroom hats on the heads
of a new progeny of statues, of Agent Orange
in mourning dress, of tomahawk fins
as they leave a child's eyes
open forever.

Think,
think,
perhaps the letters of those who drowned,
who are dizzy for a tuft of grass and a drop

of water, who are lepers in the womb,
stiff as nails in long lines for a brittle moon,
that so-called loaf of bread,
perhaps their letters are still moaning
in bottles the waves of the two oceans keep
on tossing back and forth.

FJ

Dog's Tail

My mother died in 2000 after she learned that all the clocks and calendars had changed, and possibly after she heard about something called "the millennium." Although she was illiterate and had no need for complex numbers, she knew, perhaps because she was preparing to depart it, that the world would not change because of mixed-up clocks and calendars. Her guide on this point was her favorite Bedouin proverb. In the parable, a dog's tail is placed in a mold to straighten it, but it emerges as crooked as it had ever been when it is pulled out forty years later. A parable, which it so happens, perfectly encapsulated my mother's opinion of me!

KM

03–03–03

The day, according to rumor, that the old bearded man with Middle Eastern features admonished an English girl not to take the subway, after she handed him back his wallet that had fallen off him, that day passed without menace.

The sequentially paved threes, a rendezvous struck with the devil's instruments, were, at the end of the matter, no more than a banal numerical omen.

Otherwise, that day, as an electronic sign by the municipality of Hammersmith on King Street indicates, is just another Londoner day.

A day shorter than an Arab's joy, with a temperature of eleven degrees Celsius, a usual sky of an ashen-gray dome, and the automatic doors of Kings Mall that open and close like startled eyelids, while policemen, in their black uniforms and pointed caps, as if they had just stepped out of a cheap tourist pamphlet, shoo away a homeless man about to urinate in front of River Island's shopping window, as a bored traffic cop issues a citation to a Volkswagen van, seventies model, with a large spray paint on it that reads "No to War," parked on the yellow line.

03–03–03, Monday (which is also the third weekday in the Arabic week), is just another day in London:
I did not fall in love,
Resurrection didn't happen,
bin Laden didn't strike again,
Palestinians are still on TV screens in Dixons
carrying on their suggestive death,
Bush and Blair are competing for who's got the longer
incisors, and the world, as Wallace Stevens said, is ugly
and people are sad.

FJ

Something like Anger, like Betrayal

Even after all these years an anger that resembles betrayal fills him when he remembers her. Passions that blazed then extinguished, and the expectations that bloomed then floundered, would not shake that cursed feeling from him.

What would have happened had he not told her that he wished to end their affair because he could not return, without averting his eyes, his child's silent and persistent gaze? The boy had tried to discern his father's plans after his frequent absences from home, and after the parents began to sleep in separate rooms. He wanted to know why he walks to school with his father *or* mother, not with both holding him, and swinging him the whole way through his grade school years with the strong enzymes of their familial bliss.

Seriously, he thought, what would have happened had he not told her about all this?

Would she have moved after her impending divorce, as they'd planned in detail, from her city "N." to his city "L.," to be with him twenty-four hours a day, no space or time separating them, to gulp unsated from the springs of the love that burst out of each exchanged look, touch, or embrace, love which no poetry had written, and whose lightness no song had yet to hum?

Nothing remained of that love. Sometimes he could not even remember her face.

But his faltering memory (of this!) still catches him with the smell of her perfumes, the color of her underwear, the designs of her shoes, the inventive positions she took when they made love.

Anger, or, to be precise, a sense of betrayal, accompanies him now not because the springs of their love had dried up too quickly, but because she accepted the news of their separation without shock, as if he had not thrown a hand grenade at her feet that was to shudder the world and all that lived on it.

After a short while, a month or less than a month, scenes of their passionate lovemaking, the like of which he had not experienced with any other woman, began to shake off their brief hibernation. He asked a mutual friend about her.

She told him that his beloved was having a blazing love affair with some man.
"Another man?"
"Yes!"
"Do I know him?"
"Perhaps."
"Is it A.?"

She looked at him with laughing, mischievous eyes, but did not answer.
He didn't ask how it happened.
He only needed to remember that it was he who gave her, when love had anesthetized the wolf within him, A's phone number, in case she needed anything in her city of "N."

But when?
When did their affair start?
That is the question!

KM

Clay Tablets

for Laila Shamma‘

The first time I saw them was in a public market in Amman where the voices of bus drivers' children mixed with those of lottery ticket vendors and the grumblings of bygone souls in a Roman amphitheater. The Atlantic storm was already wearing the desert's burka and had affixed its mob into the land of the two blacks (the alluvial green and deep sorrow), and Iraqis were pouring forth, Iraqis who'd never before left their cities or Babylonian villages.

No one cared about these clay tablets. They bore meaningless signs to those who bet on quick fortunes from lottery tickets, and to the fortune-teller who tossed shells and beads on omen lines that were drawn in the sand.

You could buy one for a dinar or exchange it for a shawarma sandwich and a cold soda bottle. Yet these clay tablets, which were turned over by flat hands of women dressed in black and tattooed from forehead to chin, possessed an innate threatening force.

I contemplated one of the tablets at length, I put it close to my nose, just as those women dressed in black did, for reasons unknown to me, and the tablet grew heavy in my hand, emitted a scent of sediment, and I got to seeing images and hearing voices I had never heard before.

I saw gods and kings with pointed beards, I saw tigers and lions roaring inside cages of pure gold, I saw manacled prisoners, musicians with bloody fingertips strumming slim strings. And I saw a brick gate enameled with two bluish camel legs (I couldn't tell if this was the sky's reflection or a girl's sigh): a gate I would touch again with my own hand, more than ten years later, in Pergamon Museum in Berlin.

A voice called to me: drop this tablet, drop it. You don't carry eternity's burden with a hand that worms will eat.

FJ

Preparing for Flight

Not old age, not even forgetfulness, but a desire to unburden herself from the faces, the voices, the details (for they are the source of the earth's gravity) led her to prepare for flight.

Was that not why she let threads slip from her hands and left them dangling? Yes, she did save her energy for the last leap that would loosen all the knots that bound her to these faces, voices, and tiresome details.

I had no other explanation for my grandmother's refusal to remember me when I sat beside her in a dusk that crawled like forgetfulness on the veranda of our house in Mafraq.

Time, a slow poison which had increased its dose to her, had promised her very little. Still, she continued to wrestle with a life she would rather forgo.

I sat on the ground close to her so that she could not avoid me. She asked who I was.

"I am Yahia."
"But Yahia is in America."
"That's Ahmad, my brother. I am Yahia and I live in Britain."
"God destroy them both! Lands of filth!"

With her head fixed on the stars, which she forbade us from counting so that warts would not grow on our hands, she seemed to remember me at last and said, "So you have come."

I told her that I come every year, but without my children this time.

"But you have no children."
"That's Ahmad. I am Yahia and I am married to Hind the Lebanese. You know her. I have a daughter and a son."

She struck her head slightly, apologizing for the mix-up, laughing for the first time from behind her thick glasses that looked like ancient telescopes, especially when she raised her head to the sky (which she did often).

"Right, right, I have grown forgetful, my grandchild."

She told the story of how I had feigned illness one hot day and made her carry me on her back from the Al-Zarqa' reservoir to our house in the army campground. And when we arrived I began to jump like a chimpanzee with my friends.

"I must have healed quickly," I said, feeling happy that she had finally caught the thread that belongs to me from among the jumbled weave of her ninety years.

My father entered the room, handed me the cordless phone, and told me that my brother was on the line. After I finished the call, she asked me to whom was I talking.

"Ahmad."

And as if I was playing a silly game that had lasted longer than it should, she looked indignantly at me and said,

"Who are you then?"

KM

The Phases of the Moon in London

She and I were talking about the weather, the rusty key that opens conversations here in London. Mrs. Morrison, our old neighbor, is the last English woman on our street, where the English had dropped off one by one since the population balance tipped toward the Asian immigrants. She said; "The London sky didn't used to be like this; it must have resembled your sky in India."

I said, "I am from Jordan," but she did not pause at my correction, which she may not have seen as a correction in the first place. In that English manner whose emotional resonance is hard to read, she continued that they too used to see the stars and follow the phases of the moon.

I was not convinced, but I played along with this game of English politeness. I said, "Why did the stars and moon disappear, and what caused the sky to turn into a blotted sheet even on these nights clear as a rooster's eye?"

"I don't know," she said. "Maybe the change in the weather, or our insatiable consumption of electricity, this excessive urbanization. We light the earth and the sky disappears. You're probably better off in India."

"In Jordan," I said.

Again, she did not pause at my correction. She smiled and directed her small shopping cart toward her house, announcing the end of a conversation that politeness had imposed on two neighbors who otherwise try to avoid each other when they meet at the door.

I wanted to tell her that the skies of eastern cities, bent under military rule and corruption, are also blotted out, and that the stars that freckled our childhood with comets have also disappeared, but I feared to lose the only gift for which she envied me.

KM

Mimicking Mark Antony

The Café

The retired stage actress arrived at the scheduled time, wearing white linen pants and an engraved blue blouse that bared her dark glistening arms into two polished spears, her gaze one hundred eighty degrees around the café, as if she were looking at a missing audience.

She saw me sitting at a small table in the middle of customers who, under a sudden wave of heat, stirred their boredom with long cappuccino spoons, as I stared at her countenance with a heart that was not the wiser, so she walked toward me: dark, taut, reactionary, just as I saw her in her last play before she ran away from the ferocious sun of the East in the role of a Canaanite queen.

The only new thing about her was her hairdo, raised in a bun, on a head of calculated motions, like a lotus flower that has just opened.

I said (as my heart said something else): You look different. She said: Not at all.

And she recalled how once an Italian man she had never seen told her he had seen her in a different place (and I said to myself: An apparent man's excuse to strike up a conversation with a woman), and how later he recognized, despite failing to recall the place, that she looked like Nefertiti.

. . . .

She didn't look like Nefertiti, but like Cleopatra (I wasn't sure which role she was playing at that moment), Cleopatra who drove Mark Antony (who was trying to touch her long fingers that were tinkering with sugar packets in Im-het Café while she examined the customers' faces) to swallow a slow incurable poison.

The Street

The United Nations street was empty except for a policeman who was fighting sleep against the heat wave that makes any sleep a depressing task in a pedestrian-free street.

The miracle I had planned, in the flawed operating room of my head, at a table that separated our two anxious selves, occurred on its own.

The hand with long fingers that kept tinkering with sugar packets in a café whose customers stirred their boredom with long cappuccino spoons suddenly held my hand. The fire that erupted did not prevent the policeman from pursuing his nap.

The poison that Mark Antony swallowed in a despairing love story began to take effect.

The Party

The host was busy preparing the dishes.
His young girlfriend was busy helping him.
Some guests were busy with the rhythm of the girlfriend, who thought her boyfriend, the host, was busy with the retired actress, while other guests were busy with the small details that differentiate what's Roman from what's Greek.

The stagnant air outside was busy with the secret of the sudden heat wave.

And by the steps of the house that was busy with the scent of eastern jasmine that was busy with two ghosts who were breathing heavily in the dark, Cleopatra, who licked her fingertips that had been tinkering with sugar packets in a café where customers stirred their boredom with cappuccino spoons, was busy making sure that the sweet poison her lips had planted on Mark Antony's lips had been completely absorbed.

FJ

An Ordinary Conversation about Cancer

for Salih al-Azzaz

Whenever we recalled a friend who passed we also remembered that cancer took him.

"Does anyone these days die of anything except cancer, that cursed hunter of reveries?"

I said this to a friend who had told me about another friend upon whom cancer had crept as he was contemplating a theory of desert life. Our friend suddenly felt an unusual headache and was taken to the hospital, where they found a tumor in full command of his brain. After it was removed, he was subjected to chemotherapy, which sheared his scalp, eyebrows, and eyelashes and left him looking like a sick infant. Staring at those around him, he died silently, still not believing the whole affair, which started with "a slightly excessive" headache. It dragged him into himself, while outwardly he was fit and full-limbed.

My friend fell quiet, then said, "Did you know that my older brother died of cancer at forty?"

I told him about my mother, and how cancer had ambushed her twice: once at fifty, but withdrew allowing her ten more years. She then wrestled with it for seven months without any detectable hope. "The problem—I don't remember where I read about it—is that a person usually dies the way his close relatives die," I added.

I thought I saw him touch his head, and assured him that since he'd passed forty this rule should not apply to him. As for me, the possibility is still tuning its strings before me.

He asked me how I'd like to die.

With a heart attack, I said, asleep in my bed, and in the morning they'd find me dead.

He agreed; a heart attack is the quickest and least humiliating way to die, he said. He didn't have his brother's courage who refused chemotherapy, kept his full head of hair, and smoked and drank until his last gasp.

My friend fell quiet again, slightly longer this time. "Are you sure people die the way their close relatives die?"

"I am not sure," I answered.

*

I am also not sure that poets can prophesy their death, even though César Vallejo did die in Paris on a rainy day, exactly as he predicted in his poem "White Stone, Black Stone." I predict in this poem that I will die in London on a rainy day (what a far-fetched prophecy!). And I decree that I be buried in Mafraq next to my mother, who was convinced that no space will ever contain us both. Of course, she may be right, since as everyone knows, she's going to heaven.

KM

Neighbors

I

The people of Spring Grove Crescent did not need to see the sign in italicized red letters saying "SOLD" to know that Mrs. Morrison, the only Englishwoman in our neighborhood, had just moved. It was enough to see her windows without their white curtains, which in the past, opening slightly, would let you know that the old woman persisted at her daily work of keeping a wary eye for those who roamed the streets without any purpose, or those who obliviously parked in front of her doorway in the spot reserved for her only daughter—a daughter who came only on Saturdays, accompanied by a fat husband carrying a case of beer.

Those of us whose houses ringed the cul-de-sac became certain of her departure by peeking at her garden. It used to be trimmed like the mustaches of her last husband who had died of cancer two years before (his mustaches went back to the last days of the British Empire). Soon after she left, the lush plants began to disappear one after the other, like the English from West London.

II

The only problem Mrs. Morrison and I had—not to mention that I used to unintentionally lean hard on her wood fence, and that the smell of barbeque on rare summer days used to waft from my garden to hers—the only problem was that I could never convince her that I was not from India, but rather from a place that never offers any good news about the shape of the world. After that day, September 11, I was thankful for my failure in this regard. It shielded me from her alert but invisible eyes behind the white curtains.

III

Mrs. Morrison wasn't her name. I called her that so that I'd have a name for the side of the bed I slept on, between her and Mrs. Sharma on that cul-de-sac barren of stars. In fact, I never knew her name, despite our regular exchanges of pleasantries from our respective doorways. We always envied her garden, which stood between us, we who only thought of cattle and sheep whenever we saw a patch of green.

The few Christmas cards we exchanged were addressed "To Next Door Neighbor."

KM

The Stars of London

One breath after another, the days shove me forward. Lagging behind, my eyes still hunt for the sign that appeared to me as I lay on the rooftop of our house one night in Mafraq. I was counting the stars, careless that warts would burst through my hands for measuring the sky's bounty, when the sign appeared to me.

My eyes have trailed that sign ever since. It is said the sign points to a spring that leads to a slope where there is a bough and a snake. Under the bough there is a key. The key is for a dark room never to be opened. In it lies a box with a shell inside of it. And inside the shell a piece of paper reads, "Do not look for me in what looks like me, in shape or surface. For all that is shaped like me is not me, and what looks like me is not myself. I am not close or distant, but my sign is closer to you than your own jugular vein."*

One day I saw this vision and forgot the sign. Or was this told to me by a passerby inserting a needle in another needle's eye? Was he the one who spent a night in my family home and left never to be seen again?

Every night, I rest my head on the pillow in vain. I empty my eyes from the spoils of the day and cleanse my heart from the moss of a false pulse, all in hope of luring that intractable sign.

In a popular café in Old Fez, in another time or in another life, I may have heard a Moroccan saying to his agitated friend:
Don't look for the sign.
Don't stand in its way.
Don't go rummaging for it in ruins and caves.
Don't chase after stars that have misguided lovers and shepherds before
       you.
The sign does not come to you from where you expect,
and not in any way that you can imagine.

*The quote refers to a verse from sura Qaf, Quran 50:16: "And We have already created man and know what his soul whispers to him, and We are closer to him than his jugular vein."

129

In London I live wearing the face of an imaginary person, fleeing my mother's prophecy in which my given name rings like a disturbing memory. "Yahia," she cries, "your soul will never touch comfort." And of course, she was right. Here it is nearly impossible to lie on the slanted roof of your house, trying to count the stars that have deserted their posts.

KM

Cavafy's Mask

As his young poet self thought one rung
in poetry's long ladder is a trivial thing, I too
visited Cavafy's house one day.

The poet's Alexandria with its Hellenic mask lives
only in poems, but the extra candle that used
to light up aesthetics' youthful face and erect torso
in the pagan museum continued to dance
in a book I had just read.

Quickly, like my passing through meaning, not images,
I cast a glance on his three corners—the bar that intoxicates,
the church that absolves, the hospital where he dies—
but I only saw parables talking in morals.

I walked down a street, two streets, and thought of love's
pounce on Mark Antony's heart, and of Cleopatra's
moods toying with heads and spears.

At an elderly Alexandrian's shop, whose name
is Qaddureh, I had some fish and then digested it,
or as Egyptians say about earthly pleasures,
apprehended it, with some ink-dark tea.

At that moment, the youth I was, who never reckoned
the turtle of days would overtake his winged steps,
imagined Cavafy a stubborn crone standing in a corner
that veers slightly from the universe.

Early and traveling from one city to another, his poem
"The City" chased me like a prophecy, a worse omen
than my mother telling me my soul will never know
rest no matter how long time takes
or places change their features.

Then I forgot Cavafy, his house, my mother's prophecy,
and forgot Qaddureh (though not his fish), and still
a chisel hidden in forgetfulness's night (which is life
itself) kept on, with small rhythmic strokes,
excavating my fortress from within and without.

For no reason I went back to reading Cavafy, recalled
his house, the extra candle's dance, the ancient remnants
of Alexander's great cosmopolitan city, and understood
what hadn't lent itself to me before: his blossoming
youthful poems whose bodies darted the night
as if meteors, and the gloom of his elderly ones who hid
under skin that time had preyed upon.

The Greek foreigner, assessor of canals and dams, appeared to me
as one who disguises himself in Egyptian clothing he despises
by day, and wriggles in their pungent masculine scent by night,
imploring, in a funny Arabic, a coachman, a waiter, or some
base character, to kindle the fire of his tilted lust
(like his stance) that leads him, humming, into the ground.

. . . .

It's the night, Cavafy,
the night,
where the promised lightning of lust violates the day's
chaste mask.

You'll tell yourself, This is the last night,
the last dessert in prison
before I rip out the heart of this night that drags me
by the collar,
there will be another road,
another life.

But you won't do it.
Night after night you will walk the same steps
in the same alleys
dragged by the scruff of your neck,
without escape
or path.

It's the night,
sin's perfume, the Calypso
of those who search for any road, any sail
toward home.

Ghosts dance in the dark.
Horns and contrabasses lure desires
that gape at the mouth whenever you toss them
a piece of your flesh.

It's the night.
It will find its way to you wherever you are,
so ready yourself to bid it farewell
as Mark Antony, with daring anguish,
bid Alexandria farewell.

FJ

New Uncollected Poems, 2008–2014

Petra: The Concealed Rose

I

We know you're hiding there
behind that rib cage of a guard.
Breathing with the mountain's lungs and watching,
through the rock's sunken secret,
comers and goers who are seduced by descriptive talk,
before silence stamps its lilac seal on their lips.

Without a compass we know where you are.
We know your writhing path
like a pain in the waist.
We have often visited you.
Entered the labyrinth and cave.
Bent this way and leaned another.
A swift light fell on us
as darkness followed darkness in the blink of an eye.
How many times were we led by step and yearning and dry throat
in a pilgrimage that resembles wandering in your parts?
Whenever we thought we had reached your limit
we found ourselves at the limbs of your story again.

No one is exempt from this when he sees you:
rubbing his eyes in your patient morning, you redhead Bedouin.

We will read about you in more than one language.
And bring along an expert guide in antiques
or a magician specialized in astronomy and amulets.
We will use sound probes, infrared rays, carbon dating.
We will join excavation circles, join rhetoric and curiosity, and distribute the
tasks.
But we won't make headway into the camouflaged hide
of your name, body, and story.

It isn't easy to cross the chasm to the place where your name, not the one
we call you by, was born complete, and your ankle gleamed
like the corolla of a black iris.

The advanced equipment we carry is not enough,
the maps we unfold on the ground are not enough
yet childhood might lend a hand:
we stuck our ears against an urn or a wall.

We spotted a ceramic jug in an excavator's hands.
Oil was leaking from the find recovered from the ruins.
The plant was green.
The bird was green.
And the Bedouin song on camelback, which is no longer heard
around here, reverberated faintly on both sides of this forsaken place.

By the chasm's rim, rock and spell embrace.
We can't tell which sheltered the other through time.

This silence that dominates, after the infection of speech,
is not tongueless. Familiar emptiness doesn't mean void or nothingness.
There are creatures who continue their secret lives in this seclusion
and voices whose frequencies aren't picked up
by the sensitive devices we wield.

You have a lot of lovers and a heart that beats from five directions.
The lovers did not leave much talk behind,
only urns that have cracked under the drought's sun.
The lovers used to talk through flute and chisel
before they dispersed in the lands.

We explain this as follows:
you didn't leave your wadi or abandon your gods,
your lovers did, when caravan and dirham took up another custodian.
Just like that . . .

When the road changes, the finds the road promised us retreat.
Above ground or under, the road doesn't pass through here anymore.
It hid behind the aged mountains.

You closed up on yourself.
Your rose returned to its cup.
Suns, moons, and winds succeeded nonstop
over rocks that once upon a time
were worshipped gods and sought idols.

II

This endless rose,
branching rose
that breathes with mountain lungs,
was not buried under the sand.
Was not unknown to those who remained residents between its ribs
or to those who roamed barefoot in the land.
The reasons for the lack of news about the place can be found
in the cycles of the seasons, in the changing of the road,
in discovering other paths for commerce and robbery,
and perhaps in the vanishing that has acquired lineage and prayer.
For nothing glistens under this drought's crackle
save thirst and mirage and the seclusion
whose chant is played on a single string.
And there were those who waited for the Sick Man's last breath,
the one who took a long time to die under his red fez,
under the tughra that resembled a coiled grape cluster
or a winged mast.

And there are others who remained near Musa's spring,
who know what glows behind al-Siq:
the Liyathnah know more than one entry to the concealed city,
besides the one cleft in rock that narrows and widens
for the seemingly eternal dance of light and shadow.
Despite all this, it was written for Johann Burckhardt, the Swiss,
to be the first to parade the news of the concealed wonder,
this magnificent rocky rose lurking behind the mountain,
back to the map keepers in the metropolis.
Petra is not new to the Liyathnah and Rafaieh,

to the Nueimat and Howeitat
and other Arabs of the mountains
that surround the wadi like a rib cage
or a tasseled talisman to guard eternity.

III

There are some who dwell within its caves.
And some who reside inside that rose womb.
There are pilgrims that ascend to Haroun's tomb
and present live offerings to him, Musa's brother
who had no speech impediment.
There are lively goats grazing grass below al-Deir,
and shepherds who detect, with hawk eyes,
a water hole near Wadi al-Seer.
The Swiss himself saw traces of the offerings
on piles of ritual stones, on his way to the tomb of this prophet
that Islamic folklore has adopted as patron.
The blood of offering renews under a sun that peels the scalp.
Burckhardt never reached the tomb.
He wasn't interested, to begin with.

That was his pretext to enter the wadi of the present-lost
rose he wanted to tell the "world" about.
He wanted to see with his own eyes
what he heard from the Bedouins about the wadi's marvels.
He wasn't the kind who'd believe in the oral history of such people,
their tattered and flimsy metaphors are neither news nor science.
They exaggerate their trifles
and don't care about what's worthy of attention and research.
For them, aesthetics are to be eaten, drunk, and utilized.
They can spot a dry plant a mile away but can't see the sun
slowly setting like a blood orange behind the horizon.
Rifles excite them more than an obelisk or a black iris.
This is a broken record Western travelers would repeat,
from Johann Burckhardt to Wilfred Thesiger.

Burckhardt hadn't equipped himself for a meeting like this.
He wasn't after any "discovery" here.
The "discovery" that originally set him on his Syrian travels was far.
But this journey was merely an arduous anthropological exercise,
and error or chance or veering off the trodden path
is what put him face-to-face with a "discovery"
no European had beaten him to.
And since he possessed no identifying papers,
and since he appeared suspicious to the patrolmen of warring governors,
the Swiss feared Mohammad Ali Basha's soldiers
who were stationed in Aqaba, and opted for a strenuous path
to reach Cairo: he wanted to cross the Sinai in a straight line
starting from Wadi Musa. It was difficult for him
to enter the wadi alone even if he had worn
Arabic clothes, called himself Ibrahim bin Abdullah,
and pretended to be a gunpowder manufacturer from the village of Adma.
To begin with, he doesn't know the area.

The accuracy of certain narrations about the wadi's marvels
are difficult to ascertain: transient infidels,
treasures guarded by the spell of jinn
where it's possible for a wizard like himself
to assertively command the riches to follow him
in the air invisible to all other eyes.
But because he didn't want to appear in a wizard's costume,
and more as a man who had solemnly pledged to keep his vow,
he hired a new local guide, not the one he was provided in Huweitat.
The new guide who would accompany him to fulfill his vow refused
a fee less than two horseshoes.

IV

Burckhardt could have passed by it a thousand times and not seen it.
Just as he passed by Qusayr Amra and said he didn't see images
of humans or plants on its walls.
He would see soaring, arid mountains

burrowed and furrowed by wind, rain, and tempest.
And a liaison sun whose ferocity he would underestimate
since he had never been to the place in summer.
Indeed, it was summer, the hottest part of summer.
And he felt as if he was suffocating when he reached al-Siq.

What is a Swiss man masquerading
in Arab dress to see here?
Mountain paradigms of drought's brutality.
Barely a plant grows here, barely a bird flies.
Humans scattered in the lowlands clash
over sprouts and water drops.
Not much to see or to lust after.
Lowlands, thirst, tremors.
Unless one has heard something from nearby Bedouins
it is impossible to know what those mountains hide.
Even if one approaches the city via the nearest mountain
he wouldn't see a thing. Nothing
prophesies what's behind a rocky cage
taut over a faint pulse.

V

The first sign eyes the Swiss man
as he descends to Wadi Musa with steps
an invisible magnet pulls downward.
There will be a spring burst out of rock,
trees and plants that have sprouted and wrapped themselves with the force
of creation water gives to a dead seed:
oleander, bramble, cane, and maybe some figs, grapes, and poplars.
He will continue his descent until he reaches a declivity
that flattens at the outskirts of the concealed city and runs
into a high rock wall . . .
How was he to anticipate, had he been without a guide, within these rocks
that lean one against the other,
the presence of something he had never seen?

But the Swiss who calls himself Ibrahim bin Abdullah
knows something, and he may have felt a shudder within his chest.
Some stories he heard from the Bedouins
about the sealed treasure city on his way to Cairo.
It's true he didn't fully trust their narrative
because he doesn't trust the tales of natives,
but some invisible magnet led him downward.
This time he had to believe those stories,
had to have faith in metaphor even if it was tattered,
something within his guts, a heavy intuition.
Something whose force was irresistible pulled him downward.
Ibrahim bin Abdullah does not usually abandon his wolfish caution.
But no, this time he would, a little.
What he was about to encounter deserves a gamble
and maybe even veering off the path.

VI

We'll leave Burckhardt who knew nothing about this concealed city before
his strenuous journey. We'll leave him right here. At the quake that hit him,
after the long dance of light and shadow in al-Siq, and while watching the
sudden burst of beauty one man alone cannot bear. And what's worse, here
was a professional reporter who couldn't dare to unsheathe his pen on paper
in front of the local guide who doubted how genuine his offering to the
prophet Haroun was. What Burckhardt said later was from a memory trained
on description and taxonomy. But before we leave Burckhardt or Ibrahim
bin Abdullah or Ibrahim al-Shami, we, who frowned upon expeditions
and foreign travelers in those suspicious days, must acknowledge the man's
courage, curiosity, and even some debt to his detailed report. The word
"Orientalism," which has the ring of an insult between us, shouldn't blind
us to justice. Thus we can say to Burckhardt or Ibrahim bin Abdullah as we
leave him here: Thank you. Not because you discovered this secret beauty, but
because it shook you in a manner you couldn't bear, and you started talking as
if you were hallucinating or reciting poetry. Another narrator would take over.
I mean, hallucinate like a poet. He could be any one of us, we the visitors of

this intentionally concealed city. In reality, we are in no need of an author or a poet. Anyone who enters the city would speak the same words. Tone might differ, but speech is one. Because it isn't the speech of man, but that of the present-lost carved out of a mountain's rib, a female rib, in fact. It isn't necessary to wear imagination like an ornament. What's one's need for it here?

VII

The winding longitudinal crack
in the immense rock wall
conceals the city from sight.
This isn't the first sign to the city,
it isn't even a sign.
It's a lost path
that infiltrates a mountain's gash.
And we wonder what *siq* means?
Is it from *siyaqeh*, to lead or guide?
Or is it from *shaq* or *tashaquq*
meaning crack, tear, or fissure?
No definite answer.
And it might be *shiq*, half or doppelgänger.
It might also simply be *line*.
But let's examine the Bedouin word *ziq*:
the collar hem of a woman's dress.
Which brings to mind what a Bedouin woman said
in anger to her recalcitrant son:
You want me to tear my *ziq*?
She was holding her dress from the neckband
with both hands as if she were about to split it in half.
Nabataean, Arabic, or Bedouin worlds are not separate worlds.
Here the tongue is a museum of words.
But enough of the dialectic of language,
it is of little import now.

VIII

There are many other signs that should be seen by what's beyond sight.
Perhaps with the palpitation that precedes the event.
Perhaps with touch and closed eyes.
But for those who have no vision, in a myopic time,
there are small, scattered signs attainable with sight.
Some carvings. Small seals chiseled in stone.
And of course, we'll see a few graves outside the city's inner quarters.
They belong to the upper classes
whose names are written.

. . . .
. . . .

Then we enter al-Siq.
That's the path we know even though
there are other known paths
by those who claim a lineage to the city.
We don't know the truth of their lineage
since many have come and gone.
And names change here as they do elsewhere.

IX

Early signatures of what awaits us in this wandering pilgrimage
will be met in al-Siq. The signs prepare us,
with cunning and seduction, for the ensuing shock.
A feeling of suffocation will alternate with one of relief.
The air can be completely still,
standing over the head like a mass,
and it can
suddenly rise
like a fan.

The water that tells of life
also tells of the place.
Those canals that used to deliver clear water
from springs that burst outside the city,

we will soon see them, almost as they were,
except they are dry now.
That's what killed the city, that was
its Achilles' heel.
It wasn't difficult for the invaders
who had to pass by Musa's spring to recognize it
as the city's public secret.

X

From now on all metaphors
that come to mind are possible.
Especially the feminine ones:
al-Siq / al-Shaq
the womb
the pink transparent flesh
entry
tightness . . .
and the crowning shudder: al-Khazneh.
For those who don't like sensory synecdoche
they can see its opposite,
the speech of Sufis:

Let the rock wall facing us be
"the veil,"
let al-Siq be the "path" of the "seekers"
and let our arrival to al-Khazneh, after fatigue, be
"transfiguration"
or the concealed made apparent.

XI

Before the sudden rose bloomed in front of us like a desert dawn all at once,
we had no clue as to where and to what al-Siq would lead us.
Al-Siq says, be patient,
persist for your eyes and feet

to deserve this journey's fatigue.
The road will lengthen between light and shadow,
sky will disappear then gesture,
yet the journey isn't without a guide.
Stare at the high fissure above,
the shocking fissure,
and you might see.

XII

Light descends on us like a tongue of fire.
Al-Siq quickly shelters us with damp shade.
We walk and walk into successions of fire and shadow
without knowing when we might arrive.
We will know, without a doubt, this great fissure in the mountain
is not man-made, or at least not most of it.

Its wrinkles and bends,
widening and narrowing,
roughness and softness,
spaces and masses,
all can be a mesmerizing knockout blow
by nature's hands, and some even say by jinn.
Still, without a doubt, we will
appreciate the cunning plan of those who made it
into an impossible entrance
to their concealed dwelling.

XIII

First al-Siq, then the city.
We are not sure of this order.
But it will occur to us that without al-Siq
there'd be no city.
It's one of the city's secrets, maybe
its origin point. Impossible

for the invaders to pass through this narrow
winding passage and remain alive.
First they'd have to know
the city's weakness: water.

Spells and signs, revered by the people of the concealed city,
accompany us, look out on us from the rock then disappear
before we reach the complete works.
Rock betrays some of the concealed secrets
but does not fully disclose them.
Here disclosure is prohibited.
Dangerous.

XIV

There are some drawings of certain deities near the water.
The holy embrace the holy.

But water is only a dewy memory in the canal's imagination.
There you'll find Dhu-Shara, with a face that speaks
of early creation, next to al-'Uzza: son and mother
glistening like two calm stars in the labyrinth.
There are also traces of giant camels and cameleers
in rose rock that greet the desert ships
and their captains.
Still, al-Siq reveals only a little,
a preface or a threshold,
a stoic exercise in patience;
after a long play between light and shadow,
searing and moisture,
choking and salvation,
boredom and yearning,
pungent fig odor and animal excrement,
we are face-to-face with shock:
al-Khazneh.

XV

From the last bend in al-Siq, part of the concealed wonder appears. Then
we see it whole, radiant, a gigantic studded rose, a souvenir from the age
of giants. If we see it from afar (the opposite side, for example) we will
see a carving, a small ring in the great mountain where it was dug out.
But if we stand below it we will see only it. The mountain will disappear,
as will corrugations and creases, and the soil that falls dead from drought
then remains, alone, as mistress of presence and surface. We will think this
enormous carving is endless: its six rosy ribs, Corinthian ornament, royal
crowns, and poppy mornings, all guarded by Egyptian, Greek, and Arab
deities: Isis, Aphrodite, al-'Uzza. Three different names united by the holy
feminine in one mold. We will stand below it and won't see the mountain,
and will say in awe: How could a bunch of Bedouins (one of the narratives
on the city's origin claims they were land pirates, road bandits) achieve this
wonder that perplexes language and turns imagination into a crawling child?
A young local guide will tell us he doesn't exactly know how the Nabataeans
transformed from the nomadic phase to being makers of an elegant
civilization. But he knows they were the ones who built al-Khazneh and other
sites in this rose city. They used to chisel from top to bottom, he says. We step
a few meters back to see the beginning up top, as the guide explains. It seems
easy when explained. Then we notice our short, dwarfish statures in front of
the pillars, and are not convinced. Easier to believe the myth: that the builders
of this giant monument, carved in rock with alternating colors, were jinn. We
will see small pits, depressions in the upper part of al-Khazneh, and the guide
will say they were likely pivot points for the wooden scaffolds used in carving.
Or for the workers to steady themselves with their feet. No one entirely knows
the function of these small holes, left now as witness and puzzle for visitors.
We will also see, if this isn't our first visit to the city, a new thing beside al-
Khazneh, by its threshold, under an iron lattice. Some excavation taking place.
We will look through the lattice window and notice al-Khazneh's shadow.
Is that its shadow? Of course not. It seems it is the royal cemetery. So this is
the temple, the sanctuary, or mausoleum, or I don't know what, at which the
Bedouins fired their rifles, at its upper receptacle to be exact, or so it is said,
thinking it was filled with the Pharaoh's gold.

XVI

Six sweet pillars spiral like a dessert, like "the lady's arms."
Above them another six pillars like the legs of fleeing horses.

Symmetry repeats
but dimensions vary.

The two large central pillars below are a good distance apart.
Something scraped their spiral arms, time or foul play,
without affecting their impressive sturdiness.

Gods, Amazonian women, vegetation, carnivorous birds, a mammal about to fly,
branches, human faces, a ritual chalice, geometry, solar disk, grain spikes,
the seven days, Resurrection, Judgment Day, all mingle in limitless play of
beauty.

Nothing overpowers another. Here, balance is just.
Invisible geometry grants the elements their share of the live offerings.

XVII

The merciful gods, the wrathful gods host one another.
Origin is not a problem here in Rekem,
and language doesn't stand as barrier between two guests or merchants,
they speak more than one language here
and write more than one alphabet.
Be from Egypt or Athens,
Babel or Rome, civilized or barbarian,
as long as you don't step on the city's toes,
or scheme behind its back.
Be whoever you are, but if in Rekem
do as Rekemans do.

XVIII

All who wrote about Petra imagined it as female. A pagan goddess like the morning star, a queen in a golden chariot pulled by four horses, a young shepherdess guiding a herd of goats, a Bedouin woman weaving an endless mat, a queen daughter of a queen. The feminine metaphor was ready at the tips of their pens, as it was ready at mine in discussing al-Siq. Still others, who desired to be more contemporary in expressing a femininity that is difficult to pass through with ease, wrote about a blonde tourist who rolls up her pants and wades in a captivating mirage, or an archaeologist who impersonates at night the images of ancient queens, or a student of history whose name is that of a famous Arabic lover as she guides a team of students, like a gazelle ascending to al-Deir. Yet it is possible for the sensory metaphor to flip into a Sufi ramble within one range. The sensory and the abstract merge, how wondrous, in ink. Sometimes it is difficult to tell them apart. The abstract has a roothold in the sensory, perhaps it drips in the urns of utmost desire, the impossible desire, drop by drop, until vanishing.

I ask myself: Why isn't the masculine present when Petra is present? Why are womb, tenderness, fragility, bottlenecks, rose, silk, frankincense, kohl, ankle, belly, and navel present, while sword, spear, and muscle aren't? If Petra were Roman there would have been no way to avoid the sword, shield, spear, and helmet. This is what distinguishes Petra. Its closeness is to Athens, perhaps, more than Rome. Yet Athens worships masculine beauty, boys' supple muscles, the glistening warrior flesh like the romp of a fleeing colt. Petra isn't Greek because its beauty is feminine, and it isn't Bedouin. I mean not the work of nomads searching for some vegetation and a water hole. What is Petra then? How did this branching rose sprout in an arid wadi? How could such fragile beauty conceal itself behind a scowling gruff mountain? Do settled dwellings rise like that without childhood? Where is Petra's childhood? The chisel's first strike? The stumbling gait of the entrancing young woman? This is what we still don't know with certainty. All that was written about Petra, all the chisels that dug into the layers of sand, all the experts of manuscripts and extinct worlds who flocked to it, the old dictionaries, the probes of space stations, all failed to reach this cocoon that hides the secret, or the piece of paper on which a poet claimed this was written on it:

Don't seek me in simile, for all who are like me are not me, and all who
resemble me are other than me.

XIX

Your name is Shaqila,
though some call you Shaqilat,
meaning shaqiqet al-Lat: al-Lat's sibling sister.

***

You had no statue among the chatterers in temples and halls
but perhaps it was your scent that rose
from a wide fig leaf dangling in al-Siq.

***

Those nonstop shifting colors
between al-Deir and Qasr al-Bint
may be the memory of your clothes or accessories,
or may even be your breath.

***

The eye by itself, in this place, is not considered proof.
The defendant must offer something else to the jury.
What about dream?

***

Let's suppose it happened like that:
in a brief snooze in a cave that has become an improvised café,
someone took me by my submissive hand to the gifts of the unknown
and paraded me through your palace, door
by door,
room
by room,
couch
by couch,
and perplexed

I lingered here and there
as if I had entered through the narrowest flap
and was shut inside.

***

A lilac apron carelessly tossed
on the edge of a bed of oak,
a sandal of doe skin,
a pot of ambergris,
an applicator and its kohl holder,
remnants of a lazy royal forenoon sleep.

***

You took off your clothes
your gold ring
your stone earrings
the two scorpions wrapped around your neck,
you waved to me, with the apron that received
for three intense nights, in the year of the rooster,
some rare dew, then tossed the apron my way.
The fragrance of cup flowers and juniper,
the clouds that gathered and thundered,
the grass that turned savage,
and the cane that craned.

***

I filled my hands with pinecones,
I set sleeping pigeons flying
then returned them to their nests
unlike what they were before,
I leaned on an edge,
an irrigation channel,
a well, I am not sure,
and sipped
and the more I sipped
the more I thirsted and lost my tracks.

***

This apron is for you, not for another.
I know it with my eyes closed,
by the smell of pastures,
ram and ewe,
curdled milk,
fennel and squill,
dove's-foot,
chamomile,
all of which settle and sway
within your apron.

***

With this hand I touched
the beading star,
the moon's roundness,
the snakeskin,
the recklessness of grass,
the angst of dew,
the water of life.

***

I don't possess proof of this earthly ascension of mine,
not of the unknown's grant, or of the gift of chance.
Only this hand
that returned with a map of scents and signs.

. . . .

FJ

If You're Passing through Rome . . .

Since you won't set roots and won't bend like a willow over a waterwheel, what's the use of sending vicious looks followed by piercing ones and having both end up in supplication? You won't catch more than a hand's unprompted gesture on a table, or a face that looked, unintentionally, back. Not with a stare, no matter how focused and long, or even Medusan, will you, who are passing through Rome, change the customs of Rome and its people. This here isn't a decoration of cardboard that will succumb to your obliterating gaze; touch it yourself to believe that reasons gather themselves by themselves, sometimes in an imbecilic laugh or a floral shirt. You don't have a clue, for example, why this woman, who appears like a long gasp, is hanging on the arm of an ugly man, and you don't have a clue how that planetary mass leans on a woman a breeze could blow. Not with a stare, no matter how trained, piercing, or fixated, can you turn her sugar spoon in her coffee cup. You're probably the only one who thinks that drooping an eyelash or bowing like a knight can barter with a life of flesh and blood. So when your stare returns to you eclipsed, don't say it's money, fame, or even luck. A man passing through does not leave a tattoo on an arm or a scar on a clavicle. Yet remember this, if remembering is worthwhile: that reasons have gathered themselves for you, in another Rome, into one word, one word that you don't know how it alighted on you or how you pronounced it, because the stares that were aimed at the one who had flung herself on your arm, with all her lavender load, those arrows have missed their mark.

FJ

Don't Do as Romans Do

And since no family awaits you at dinner, and there's no campaign to teach the barbarians beyond the border a lesson, what's the use of doing what Romans do? Sit in the wind corridor of arrows flying around you and observe how you'll get out unscathed, lightweight, even if the past dumped its loads into your feet. At this late hour you, who are passing through Rome, won't change what has become of the Romans, so don't marvel anymore at the swelling commotion in cafés, or at songs that glorify love not war. This is another time: trees no longer step beyond their shadows, and they don't die in poems as they used to do. And smile, if you can, to the faces of those who think life is the servant of the obedient family. When you saw the royal men steadily walking ahead of the majestic funeral, there was someone in Beirut sharing a glass of wine with a woman, while another in Timbuktu was kneeling a camel loaded with salt.

FJ

On the Way to You

She will come, the one you wove with the finest needles of patience, and you've been waiting for her appearance day after day, when all you wished for from Mister Storm, who was once an obstinate god and used to chase kings with rain and tempest, is that she doesn't arrive late. It's true that you were born in a family of longevity, your health appears, so far, good, and your body parts that you rely on when you're called to work, those you wash every morning with the water of vows. Yet life, dear son of my mother, is a reckless cylinder that doesn't hesitate about tossing any excess baggage to the road. Or haven't you seen how they ended, those who clutched on to anything that would help them arrive? She's a little late, shorter than you thought, with less wavy hair, and two or three wrinkles around the lips, no biggie, no worry, these things are to be expected on her long journey to you.

FJ

By Chance as Well

Even if you did say that chance was your life's heroine, that she is the one who delivered you almost whole to a city many before you had reached, you only captured her with your pen name whose lack of blood type did not raise anyone's suspicion, and also with your tricks, which you learned at an early age in the villages of heat and dust, when your mom realized that a drooping shoulder won't gesture to the star of bliss as it distributes titles and fortunes to the living, which is why you grew up bent, not because of some vertebral anomaly, but because you'd heard a blind man say one day to a reckless boy that people with straight postures can't see farther than their noses, and that branches, meteors, and tears always fall down. Out of the scraps you'd picked up on the postal roads and the roads of rescue and relief, you made a protective shield for whenever sleep overcame you, to ward off whatever arrows that might find you by mistake.

FJ

Light

During her final days, which we sort of knew would be her final days, since cancer rarely pulls a prank, and the eyes of farewell often don't postpone what they want to stay today for tomorrow, my mother, watching me prepare my suitcase for the departure I came from and to which I'd return, said in supplication: "May God light your way."

In what I heard I instantly saw the Verse of Light, written in complicated Kūfic script, hanging on the wall: "God is the Light of Heavens and Earth, the parable of His Light is as if there were a niche and within it a lamp, the lamp enclosed in glass, the glass as if a brilliant star lit by a blessed tree, an olive not of the east and not of the west, whose oil is luminous without a flame having touched it: Light upon Light . . ."

In which darkness did my mother see my way, so that she'd spend a few more of the precious words she had remaining in her account? What did her eyes that gleamed with the glow of extinguished silver see, as she was peering into the afterlife?

It was daylight.

The sun had granted creatures amplified shadows.

An old saluki dog sat panting under a eucalyptus tree.

Pebbles were incandescent in a dry riverbed.

It was no ordinary light that my mother wished to illuminate my path. It wasn't Edison's lightbulb, or fluorescent, luminescent light, or the light of projectors at football stadiums, or that of the space shuttle's orbiter. It wasn't Shakespeare's pendulum in no-man's-land, between light and lightness. It wasn't even the Pharisee torch that Christ set aside. My mother meant *noor*. Although she was likely ignorant of the argument that still rages on in Arabic about the difference between the two lights, *noor* and *dau*.

Astronomers, obsessed with their observatories and mathematics, say there is no scientific difference between *noor* and *dau*, that they are no more than poetic wordplay. But Sufis claim a difference that observatories can't detect and math can't comprehend. God, the Light of Heaven and Earth, doesn't need to resort to a game of words and meaning to resemble poetry. Yet even so, there is no harm if *noor* is poetry and *dau* is prose, since the latter has numerous sources, and dances according to supply and demand. The former, however, like poetry, is rare. If and when *noor* is revealed to one, that person will survive many an unseen darkness. And the veil may even be lifted and one might become a saint.

Years have passed since my mother's death. I no longer resemble my Bedouin ancestors and look to the stars during my stays and travels. For all I know, only batteries and electric companies have lit my way.

It's clear, for reasons I can guess, that God did not fulfill my mother's prayer.

All this came to mind while I was trying, unsuccessfully, to write a poem about a greenish light, lime luminosity, limelight, citric light that leaves no shadow of an outstretched hand or a body walking in its domain.

Is remembering my mother a pretext to write about *noor/dau*, or is writing about them a pretext to remember my mother?

Dau will be the last thing humans see.
The origin
is the dark.

Behind his shut lids
a child sees *dau*.
The first thing wasn't a scream.

When we turn off *dau*
the jet-black night isn't far away.
In a flash it returns.

Under a green moon-*dau*
I extend my hand.
A willow branch shakes.

Stars and planets
aren't lanterns for our sake.
They have other tasks.

The Yemeni Sirius
is in his constellation.
An abandoned god.

Without *dau* there is no color.
Black and white
are a division of labor.

Dau and shadow are side-by-side
as long as
we remain earthbound.

Purity.
Before this visual contamination.
Your face.

Although *noor*
is essence it is
also form.

The humility
of *noor*'s essence turns it
into form.

When you are in the land of *noor*
take off your footwear,
walk barefoot as you were born.

Noor is a laughing face.
A hand waving from a distance.
Memory of mother.

FJ

"Light" was in response to a piece by James Turrell.